T0209085

REFLECTIONS
on
SUFFERING

REFLECTIONS
on
SUFFERING

MARY FAITH

REFLECTIONS ON SUFFERING

iUniverse books may be ordered through booksellers or by contacting:

iUniverse
1663 Liberty Drive
Bloomington, IN 47403
www.iuniverse.com
844-349-9409

Because of the dynamic nature of the Internet, any web addresses or links contained in this book may have changed since publication and may no longer be valid. The views expressed in this work are solely those of the author and do not necessarily reflect the views of the publisher, and the publisher hereby disclaims any responsibility for them.

Any people depicted in stock imagery provided by Getty Images are models, and such images are being used for illustrative purposes only. Certain stock imagery © Getty Images.

ISBN: 978-1-6632-1204-7 (sc)
ISBN: 978-1-6632-1206-1 (hc)
ISBN: 978-1-6632-1205-4 (e)

Library of Congress Control Number: 2020921062

Print information available on the last page.

iUniverse rev. date: 05/25/2021

Margaret's letters are endearing even with grammatical errors. The errors have not been corrected for this reason.

REFLECTIONS

*M*y God, You are total love. You have given me Your love in Communion. I can never receive You too many times. You have taken away my venial sins in this Holy Communion. I am like a virgin child. I am Your very good child.

I have had many years of dryness since I felt anything in Communion. May Your will be done in my next Communion and in each day of my life, which I give to you again. Play with me. Use me for anything you want. And if my life continues in dryness, I think all will be well.

———✥———

While I was watching a comedy on television, I looked at the new crucifix over the front door and was drawn into the center. I was so dry. I had not been able to do centering prayer for years. Yet it had been a banner day. Praise, honor, and glory to you, O my God. I do not ask for consolation for dryness. I only ask that Your will be done.

I offer everything up to You, my God, from the smallest amount of suffering to the largest. Also, I offer You my joys, prayers, works, disappointments, and frustrations for the health of others. None of these compare to the bliss of Your heavenly beatitude, O God. In Your infinite goodness, mercy, and love,

You take the smallest hurt and suffering and change evil to good for others when it is offered up.

———∞———

Recently there was a terrible earthquake in India. It is thought that about thirty-five thousand lives were lost. I heard someone on a religious show say that calamities like this can be caused by You, my God. I have heard people in parishes say the same thing about personal problems. No! No! No! My all-loving God does none of this.

I believe people's personal sins affect nature and cause an unbalanced world. Didn't You say You would save a city if only ten were good? Despite the terrible atrocity of abortion and partial-birth abortions, we have so many good souls in the United States. Thank You, my loving God, that You send Mary to warn us.

———∞———

I am tempted by the devil or evil spirits. When I am tempted, I pray to St. Michael the Archangel to pray for me, protecting me and everyone else. Then my temptations go away. You are a most wonderful friend, St. Michael. Thank you. Thank you so much. How can I ever thank you enough?

God, You are so good. I am a wretched sinner compared to the graces You have given me. I have committed and am capable of committing many terrible sins, but You, my good God, always forgive me.

———∞———

Like St. Thérèse, I have wanted to be a saint for some time. The church teaches that we should all try to become saints. God will always help with the graces He sends.

I heard on a religious television show that St. Aquinas was asked how one becomes a saint, and he said, "Will it." Each day, I will it, and I grow a little each day. However, I am so *very* far from sainthood. This is a new day. Teach me, O my God, how you would want my prayer life to be.

———⟋⟋⟍———

My God, I love You, my sweet Savior. I love you, Mary, and all the angels and saints! Please, God, bless my deceased mom, dad, friends, relatives, and ancestors.

I love You, I love You, I love You, O my God. I thank You for allowing me to love You like the useless servant. He was useless because his life, powers, and good deeds were all graces given to him in the first place. You are my grace-endowing God.

I believe in the old Jewish tradition that only the unblemished lambs should be offered as a sacrifice to God. You, O God, are the good shepherd. I have been asking you for some time to take me in union with You in a pyre of love to God the Father. I am a lamb blemished in many ways by my own sins. Nevertheless, blemished as I am, take me and all my sufferings and joys.

I am praying to You for the holy souls in purgatory, everyone on earth now, and babies in their mothers' wombs. I also pray for an end to abortion everywhere, a pro-life amendment to the United States Constitution, the salvation of souls, and a list of people who have asked me to pray for them. In addition, I have been offering my sufferings up so that a friend will participate in the Mass and in the confessional. As You know, my God, I have asked You to give her sufferings to me for this purpose.

I am in pain most of the time. Give me her sufferings of mental, spiritual, and bodily pain. I know I can do more with Your help, O my God. But not my will but Yours be done. I am so grateful to You, my God, for what You have done for me. Above all, Lord, keep me humble, humble, humble! Oh, dear God, let me be burned to the core with Your love, and from the ashes, let me rise up to be burned again.

Since I had my total joint replacement on my left knee, Margaret C. has been bringing me Holy Communion three days a week. She is always on time. I became distracted about the time one day and ate something when I should have been fasting before receiving Communion. I very much wanted to receive Holy Communion, so I asked God to make Margaret C. late enough so I could receive.

Wondrous are Your ways, my good Lord. Margaret C. showed up at my front door just in time for me to receive You, my God, in Holy Communion. I thank You, thank You, thank You! I praise You! I sing alleluia, alleluia, alleluia! I love You, I love You, I love You! Amen.

For so many years, I have complained about dryness in prayer. The reason I felt dry in prayer was because I was afraid of You and what You might expect of me if I got too close to You, my God. In the back of my mind, I knew this all along. This morning, I thought, *What do I have to be afraid of?* I love You and trust You, and I will try not to run from You again.

Praise God! Oh, what a fool I have been. This is a spiritual breakthrough. Now I can begin to love and trust and abandon myself to You. I am so happy.

One year I planned on going to the Easter Vigil Mass. In the afternoon, I felt pressured by the desire to smoke in addition to using my Nicotrol inhaler, which is a healthy substitute for cigarettes. The temptation was very strong. So I did it. I decided to have one cigarette that led to another and then to two packs a day. This was one of my weakest times.

The smoking was hurting my marriage to my husband, Jack. He said it made him depressed, and he felt hurt. I tried to smoke only in the bathroom, as Jack suggested. I marked on a calendar the number of cigarettes I smoked each day.

One week, I looked at the calendar and saw that what I considered a good day in my effort to quit was only a few cigarettes from a bad day. I was like someone drowning in my efforts not to smoke. I kept thrashing around, trying to keep from going down for a third time.

I begged God to help me, and I am happy to say that, with the help of God, I am no longer a smoker. Thank You, my God and Savior! How could I not love You, my God?

The other day, I was waiting in the car for Jack. I saw a woman walking very slowly toward the car while lighting a cigarette—or more accurately, she was trying to light one. She stopped directly in front of me. In the old days, I would have asked to "borrow" a cigarette from her. She kept staring directly at me while she slowly smoked her cigarette. But I had quit just a few days before.

Then it dawned on me who this "woman" was. It was literally the devil in disguise trying to get me to take just one. I did not ask "her" for a cigarette. I knew that one cigarette would lead to more and would hurt my marriage and health. The devil walked away after a few minutes, still in disguise. Thanks be to God for showing me it was Satan before me, trying to ruin my soul as well as my health and marriage.

———— ⁂ ————

Today, upon receiving Christ in the Host, I received more than a consolation. I was calm and very much at peace. I could feel Christ's presence within me, and at the same time, I felt His presence in the room.

I went just a bit to meet His presence in the room, soul to soul. I wanted to write this down for the dry times. I only ask, O Lord, that You keep me humble, humble, humble. You are giving me all these good feelings when I receive Your body, blood, soul, and divinity in the Eucharist. It is Your doing, not mine, and I am not worthy. Oh, I feel so blessed by You. I love You. I thank You. I adore You, and I sing alleluias to You.

I am so happy. You have given me so much. I am in love with the church, and You could never give me a better gift. And aren't You worth suffering for? I have a light cross compared to so many people. You have given me so much in the sacraments and the liturgical life of the church.

I think that You, my God and love, have given me so many special blessings when there are so many people more worthy. Now I remember that You, my love, for Your own name's sake and glory, give blessings to the weak and not the strong. Yes, You, my God, use the weak to confound the wise.

———— ⁂ ————

I remember the day the World Trade Center and the Pentagon were attacked by what the United States has called terrorists. This started a new kind of war for us in America. I love my country. The mission of the terrorists was a suicide mission. They were willing to give up their lives for the evil that they believed was right. Perhaps they are in heaven for laying down their lives for their holy war, despite the loss of innocent lives.

Osama bin Laden, their leader, is alive, crazy, and well! He reminds me of Charles Manson who sent his followers out to do his dirty work. Both have a very high degree of charisma. Both are cowards. No matter what, I am not in favor of the death penalty for *anyone.* God conceived us, and He should know the length and end of life.

Monsignor has said that we might be very surprised when we get to heaven and see who is there. He believes there is some possibility that Stalin is in heaven despite the millions he killed. Monsignor told me Stalin was savagely beaten as a boy every day by his alcoholic father. I shout that we have a merciful God who is worthy of honor and praise. Our God's name is Mercy.

———— ‿ ————

When I started to tell a friend that some people might be given a second chance after they die, she went ballistic. Some months before, she had told me that Tom and his wife were going straight to hell because they had not accepted Jesus as their savior. She was not big on Catholics either. She said, "Praying to the saints is a bunch of bologna." She said she never wanted to talk to me again.

While she was still angry with me, however, I thought about our conversations and decided I did not want to lose her as a friend. I left a message on her answering machine asking her to forgive me for any un-Christian thing I had said. I did the right thing for partially the wrong reason. I should have asked her forgiveness, if any was needed, but I most definitely should have stood up for the Roman Catholic Church first. She got over her attitude, and we are friends again.

However, when she was still mad at me, I was having a terrible time keeping my hands off the phone to call her. I wanted to say to her, "If you only believe in the Bible and believe a person should strictly stay by it and nothing else, why have you been married three times? Doesn't Jesus say in the Bible that the only reason for divorce is adultery? Then, my friend, are you saying your first two husbands were unfaithful to you?"

I called Father Martin at home and told him the whole story. He and I only talked for a few minutes, but I was able to vent enough not to call her. Father Martin said, "Your friend is a fanatic, and no one can talk to anyone like her."

Josephine (who I have known since the fall of 1964 and who is a very good Christian) and I can sit down and peaceably talk religion. Jack and I can, and Tom and I can. I have been praying especially hard for my friend even though we are friends again. I hope that she will think more highly of my Roman Catholic Church.

I don't know what just happened. After finishing my writing, I finished watching a video about St. Gemma of Galgani. I turned the video off, and the television came back on as it was supposed to do. I thought, *I will put in the video of Our Lady of the Rosary in the Basilica at Lourdes.* I looked up at the television and saw flames at the bottom. I thought, *How strange.*

Of course, the video didn't have anything to do with the flames. I had just finished putting holy water on my forehead in the + and lips + and heart + and soul +, consecrating myself to God the Father (Abba), the sacred heart of Jesus, the Holy Spirit, and the immaculate heart of Mary, the Blessed Virgin. I thought when I saw the flames it might have something to do with the devil. I looked down and then up again, and the whole screen was filled with flames for ten seconds. Then the video came back on.

I don't know if the devil was trying to escape the holy water I flicked in front of my chair or if he was trying to scare me. If he was trying to scare me, it did not work. My spirit rejoices in God, my Savior! Now I will go through the decades of a videotape on the rosary.

You are the way, the truth, and the life. Keep me humble in Your truth, for humility is truth. I love You. I want to be Yours now and forever, even if I have to give up my life for You. The thought of that brings fear and questioning about how strong I will be if faced with martyrdom. If I keep my eyes on You, I do not need to be afraid of anything. For as it says in Romans, nothing can separate us. And, of course, all things come together for the good for those who love You.

Enfold me in Your love, my God. Mary, my most blessed mother, my momma, and, for the hardest times, mommy, let me stand as close to you as any child does. Lord, please give me the graces I need to love You and trust You for *everything*. Help me to love Your mother, Mary, as she should be loved.

Soon I will have a total joint replacement of my right knee. It is painful now, and that is why I am having the surgery on it, two to eight months before my left knee is supposed to be healed. Because of everyone's prayers, I have healed amazingly well, according to my surgeon. However, every time I get up or sit down, both knees hurt despite my taking morphine-based pain pills. During these times when I get up or down, I offer things up in my usual way to God. I offer my pain up to God for all His holy souls and for all who are not His holy souls yet.

My God, You have been so good to me in every way imaginable. I will try even harder to embrace the cross for the love of You. Thank You again and again for giving me the grace to want to embrace my cross. I try my best to embrace my cross in joy.

Today, I have been in so much pain. I am Mary's child, and I run to her. I lie across her lap as she strokes my hair.

I talked to Father Martin. He said I should not pray for canonization but for holiness. What is the difference? A person can be holy but not be canonized. However, a person who is canonized has already been declared holy. I think Father Martin just did not want me to order a glass case for my incorrupt body yet.

The priests at church say God wants all of us to become saints. Whatever God wants of me, I will try to discern and do to the best of my ability.

I went to confession. Instead of leaving my sins to God, when I left the confessional, I reviewed them in my mind too much. I have, however, started to rely on the mercy of God. Now, with confession, I have forgetful mercy. I am serene again. I adore You and feel Your joyful, loving presence before me.

A few days ago, I didn't know how I was going to keep leaning on You and endure all the pain. I thought my endurance was stretched to its limits. In the last two days, the pain has lessened. I am able to raise the lift chair all the way up and stand up without longing for my walker. I have been able to walk a little.

I love You and thank You with all my mind, heart, strength,

and soul. To paraphrase the Bible, You will not push us beyond our strength. I love You in faith and these concrete showings of Your great love for me. I love You, Father. I love You, Jesus (king, brother, spouse). Holy Spirit, I love You many, many times over.

I know that whatever happens to me, I can face it unafraid because You and I are one. I pray for the souls of everyone. Lord, allow all souls to find true peace and love in you. I should strive to live in the present with You, my God, and others, and to use my treasure more meaningfully in the Spirit.

———————ᴍ———————

A couple of months ago, Christ reminded me that He is everything and everything else is nothingness (material possessions). I am a small child learning to ride a spiritual tricycle. But sometimes, He picks me up and puts me on a ten-speed.

He and I ride the same bicycle in Holy Communion. He guides the cycle, in union or dryness, not me. Sometimes I am too small for the tricycle, and I wait for my loved one. Whatever happens is His will and done by Him, not by me.

Sometimes in Communion, there is dryness and sometimes union with Him. I love Him and His will.

———————ᴍ———————

I just had some evil thoughts and temptations. I am, considering the graces that have been showered upon me, one of the world's worst sinners. I can do nothing by myself, and I am not even in the same world as sainthood. But I want to be, and I believe over some course, either short or long, I will be in that ballpark and world. Of course, that is what You want for *all* of us. I am nothing special.

Just because You are close to me in Holy Communion does

not mean I am incapable of evil thoughts, words, and deeds. I do not know if I have ever been in a state of mortal sin, and yet I have committed many sins and given them to You in the confessional. I will let You decide that, as I ask in hope and trust for You to judge me mercifully. I know You want me to be in heaven and a saint exponentially more than I do.

I found out that to be a saint, a person has to live a heroically virtuous life. I wanted the sainthood without heroics. Then I started to realize that with what I had been through already in my life, with Your hand holding mine, I did not have to be afraid of anything. I did not have to be afraid of the dark days and dry nights, pain, sickness, or anything else. Nothing will be able to disturb our love as long as I persevere in our love.

How can I ever thank You for all You have done for and given me, especially Yourself, Your Mother, Mary, and the church? I am so happy in my heart that I feel like crying for joy. I love You. I will keep trying. Thank You endlessly. Thank You for Your patience with me.

All this talk of sainthood reminds me I might be having delusions of grandeur. However, nothing is impossible to God. Oh, how I love You.

The Holy Spirit, our Sanctifier, is slowly but clearly still showing me not to be so materialistic. I am very much so. God, who is everything, is teaching me that anything outside Himself is nothingness in one degree or another. Of course, all the people within the mystical body of God are separate and in union with our God. I heard a priest say the same thing. The encouragement fell on a welcoming soul.

I am selling some of my doll collection, and I would like, O Lord, to find a way to sell my diamond and ruby ring at a slight loss. It is worth about $10,000. I am selling 80 to 90 percent of my doll collection and five curio cabinets. My aim is to be more devoted to You and to help poor children.

Thank You, my love, for showing me that outside You is nothingness. Thank You for giving me the grace to sell my possessions to help others. All love comes from You. I adore You, worship You, thank You, praise You, and love You (the prayer that our blessed mother, Mary, has given to everyone in her apparitions in Fatima, Portugal, in 1917).

My God, forgive me for wasting my money and resources. I am like the prodigal son coming back to You, my loved one. If it is Your will, may the sale of my possessions bring a good price to allow me to help others. You said that there is great joy in heaven over the sinner who returns to You. Thank You exponentially for all the blessings and graces You have given me. I pray for more. I am thirsty for Your grace and love.

My God, help me so I don't fall down while I am running fast to You. I love You, my God, my Trinity, my three-in-one-person. You know how fast You want me to go toward grace. Pray for me, Mother Mary, as always.

Since the age of three years, I have had thirteen surgeries—from little surgeries like removing a big toenail to a double mastectomy. I had six surgeries in one year, including three arthroscopic surgeries on my right shoulder. I have had one major surgery on my shoulder and both knees. Believe me, I don't go near a hospital unless I must.

I also have, considering all the surgeries, offered myself as a victim to God many times. I don't know if this is fair to my husband, Jack, who helps me. If only he would convert to the Roman Catholic Church, then one day he would be canonized, because he is so saintly now. His conversion is in my daily prayer.

Once, when I was in the hospital for infected legs, I offered myself up to God to be a stigmatic. Immediately, I felt the ever-so-warm love of God cover me. What You want of me, Lord, suffering or joy, I want myself, for Your name's sake.

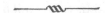

I believe I am in a state of grace. But my nature is such that I have to force myself to say one to three rosaries a day. Dearest Mother Mary, now I feel so alone, unspiritual, and abandoned by God. Pray for me, your daughter, to the Father, your Son, and your Spouse, the Holy Spirit. You are my refuge.

Father Martin says I am grieving because I am trying to change. Even though I don't feel as close as usual to God, I know I have been blessed profusely by Him. I may not be perfect physically, but I could be so much worse. He has given me many graces and the church—the church I am in love with. Thank You, my one-in-three. Thank You. Thank You.

When I look at myself, I see two completely different selves. One is like Dorian Gray's inner self. It is an old, grotesquely wrinkled, shrunken self. The other self is in a state of grace, made in the likeness of God with the Holy Trinity within, and sparkling with a multicolored, thin aura around my body.

I am watching a Catholic religious show on television about what the early Christians, the early saints, had to go through.

O Blessed Mother Mary, pray for all of us that, if called to be martyrs, we all will be equal to the faith, the church, and God. I love You. Please pray for me, your daughter, my beautiful, holy Mother.

Dear God, I will do anything for You. I will let You, my love, decide the degree of holiness I will possess when I die. I just want to do good now, and after I die, spend my heaven doing good works, like St. Thérèse of Lisieux said she wanted to do.

Please, Lord, keep me humble. Don't I know I am the worst sinner? Keep me humble, humble, humble, and may Your will be done. Even though my sins are so many, let me please serve You.

Every time I commit a sin, it hurts you and delays Your coming back in glory. And every time I commit a sin, it hurts the mystical body on earth. If I sinned less, fewer would be hurt. The same can be said of each sin and each sinner. Am I helping the abortion movement by my sins? Oh, dear Lord, I hope not.

Lord, when I see You on a crucifix, it makes me want to cry. I am so sorry, so very sorry. Oh, Lord, how I have abused You. With Your grace, I will do better.

It is a privilege to offer things up to You. Look at the company I am in when I stand on my own cross. I am standing next to Christ, our Lady, and all the saints who have stood on crosses. Oh, happy original fall from grace. Oh, Christ, *Ecce Homo* ("behold the man"), You could have saved the world and many more with one drop of Your blood. In what You went through, there is not one saint who can look to You and say, "Well, He didn't suffer what I suffer." Not one soul.

And You suffered all that You did for saint and sinner alike. Even saints commit some sins. I have asked to be a victim with and for You. But I have all the modern luxuries, even if I am in pain. I wasn't born in a stable, and I haven't had the hard life You had. How can I even thank You for all You have done for me. I have life and hope for everlasting happiness with You, my love. I have Your love and the church, and I love the church. I am in love with the Trinity, the church, and Your blessed mother, Mary.

Dear God, in Your mercy, do not forsake me, or let me ever forsake You. I love You and want to be with You forever. In Your mercy, do not abandon me. Pain throughout my body is so strong, I am sometimes tempted to question Your love. However, I still know that we will not, as Christians, be given a cross that is too much for us.

Help me, my God. O queen of heaven and my mother, Mary, pray for me. I do love you, my God. And I do love you, my mother and queen of heaven and earth. And I am sorry for every sin I have ever committed.

Today, Jesus, I was almost in tears for the suffering I have caused You. I have wept, in the past, when a priest asked me to stare at a crucifix. St. Teresa of Avila said that every Christian should weep when looking at a crucifix. My tears were real when I stared at the crucifix. I was not trying to fulfill St. Teresa's axiom.

Years ago, I asked God to make me a stigmatic but not to let anyone know until after I was dead. I have asked God to make me a victim of love. Today, I carry a mental crown of thorns. The cross on my right shoulder has been operated on twice, and there is osteoarthritis in every bone of my body, my orthopedic doctor said after looking at X-rays. In my neck, osteoarthritis has caused the development of two bone spurs, and there are two more bone spurs in the lower part of my back. The neck and back are perhaps my scourging.

Years ago, my hands were operated on for carpal tunnel syndrome. I have had osteoarthritis in my hands for some time. Now my hands are starting to curl inward slightly. I have had four operations on my knees, including two total joint replacements. Christ, while carrying His cross, fell three times.

I have had, years ago, two operations on my feet. One of these operations went well, and I was walking around in a week. After the other foot operation, I was unable to do anything for five months other than lie on the couch in severe pain. These things are my minor invisible stigmata, perhaps.

I know God has not caused these problems. I believe God saw that I would have these problems and knew my heart. He knew I would offer up my condition, and He would accept the gift.

I forgot something. I suffer from cold asthma attacks. If I am outside for ten to fifteen minutes, it is approximately forty-five degrees, and it is raining, I will have an asthmatic attack.

I believe God has said to me that I don't have to be a victim. On the other hand, that thought could be coming from my own weakness or the devil. Last night and this morning, I have reaffirmed my desire to die of love. I am *not* a masochist. I do have operations, do see doctors, and do take pain pills. I am just trying to live in the present moment with my physical problems.

Jesus, I trust in You. Other people have suffered far more than I. But this is my cross, and I carry it as best I can. Thank You, my love, for giving me the graces necessary to carry my cross, which I know is helping other souls as well. Thank You, my love, for the grace of prayerful intercession for many while in pain.

My God, I love You as much as I can, and You love me infinitely. I know I can trust You to lead me to purgatory or heaven. You will not let the cross become too much for me, as You have promised in the Bible. And I will not let anything come between us. I love You, my God, Mary, the church, and helpless others. Of course I trust in You.

———⚋———

I am very selfish, very materialistic, and impatient. I want it all, and I want it, if not now, then yesterday. However, I have been selling some of my curio cabinets and dolls so I can sponsor three young boys through a global Catholic foundation for children and the aged. For several years, I have been sponsoring Margaret in Uganda, Africa. Years ago, in a letter, I told her the best thing a woman could be would be a Carmelite nun.

The Carmelite nuns that I know intimately are very happy in their vocation. They spend their lives doing sacrifices and penances for other souls. They do not go around with sad faces. On the contrary, they laugh and tell jokes whenever they are together for recreation.

I told Margaret what the life of a Carmelite nun would be like for her. Years ago, she decided this is what she wanted to do with her life. I will tell you more about this exceptional young woman, Margaret, later.

As I have said, I am going to sponsor three young boys. These boys are from Kenya, Africa, and the boys know each other. The twenty-five dollars a month sponsorship fee for each boy covers so much. It covers food, clothing, and medical attention. It also covers schooling. For young children who become part of the foundation, it is like a dream come true. These children feel very much impressed with what they receive.

I hope to take my three young men in Kenya as far in their studies as each one wants to go. However, I will continually pray that at least one of my young men will have a vocation to the priesthood. The priests in Kenya will have, I think, an idea of which, if any, of my young men has a vocation to the priesthood. I hope God, with my hands to help, will plant the seed of a vocation in those boys who have the ability and desire to become a priest.

That seed will be given good ground to grow. I will happily sponsor a future priest. In another comparison, it will be like God and I, His servant, are taking pebbles of good works and throwing them into a pond of water (grace) in each child's soul until there are large ripples of water and grace, which become the rushing water of grace that each priest gives out in his lifetime. If my sponsored children do not become priests, there are many other grace-filled vocations in which they can do well and give out graces to others. I will be proud of them.

In the past, I have given You my mind, body, soul, strength, thoughts, words, and emotions in love of You. You are my love. Now I hope to increase all that I give to You. I also give You, in love, prayers for the holy souls in purgatory and every soul, including those people for whom I have been asked to pray. Then, of course, with You, I pray for the salvation of the souls constantly in pain.

I love You. I thank You for my endless love invitation, which began before my entrance into the church and all the graces You have given me, my love. I love You, adore You, and sing alleluia, alleluia, alleluia to You, my love.

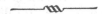

It has been my dream that someday I would be able to go to Sunday and daily Mass. Years ago, I did this and made a rough estimate of the Masses I had gone to. I thought, at the time, that those Masses would hold me in good stead for when I was old and could no longer go to Mass. I never thought my "older years" would be here now. In the recent past, I have had to stay at home and watch a Latin Sunday and daily Mass.

May God's will be done. I have arranged to buy a wheelchair van to get me to church Masses. One of my two caregivers is going to try to take me to Mass twice a week, and when he is able, to the Saturday Vigil Mass, which counts for a Sunday Mass. My pastor has dispensed me from the obligation of going to Mass on Sunday due to what he considers the state of my health. Because I am hard of hearing, I do not understand much of the Latin Mass on the television.

Unfortunately, my caregiver's only day off is Saturday. It would not be fair of me to ask him to take me to Mass on his only day off. He has two other part-time jobs and is working, he says, seventy hours a week, because he needs the money. I know he is sick now with a bad cough. He and I both feel that he is sick from the long hours he works.

How full of pride I am. God, I beg You to grant me the grace of humility. On the one hand, I am very much afraid, because Lucifer was the best and brightest angel, and he fell due to his pride. On the other hand, I ask God and Mary to pray for me every day, and who can be afraid of God and Mary in your corner?

It has been hard, very hard, to carry my cross of pain now. I am not complaining. I have been standing in the shadow of Your cross and Your crucifixion. I have gotten as close to You as I can. I want to embrace You around the lower legs, but I do not want to add to Your agony. Because I am close to You, nothing else matters, not even my pain. I am beginning "to learn of love," and

I am grateful to You and All the souls You love, which are just another personification of You.

———∽∿∽———

I became impatient with someone today over nothing. I apologized twice. I wished him a good day. He seemed pleased. I still felt guilty. Papa, Jesus, Holy Spirit, Blessed Mary, all you angels and saints, pray for and with me. I keep feeling like I must rush to sainthood. I don't know why. I have felt this often and ponder upon it.

Oh, yes, I wanted to call the Carmelite sisters and ask them to pray for Monsignor, overworked Jack, and me. Satan told me I was just trying to make myself look good to the Carmelite sisters. I dismissed him and called them anyway.

———∽∿∽———

I went to the orthopedic surgeon the other day. He said I have a torn rotator cuff on my right shoulder. He has done two surgeries on my right shoulder and two on each knee. I believe his rates are very reasonable. But, with all these surgeries, I jokingly told him one time that we were building him his summer home.

I kept pushing to go ahead and have the surgery, but Jack wanted me to put it off until later. Jack heard something that I did not hear the doctor said. The doctor said the rotator cuff surgery would be more painful than the two total-knee-replacement surgeries. I didn't feel I could stand the added pain. As I said, I am just learning to love Your cross.

I could not have the surgery anyway. For the first six weeks after, I would have my arms strapped to my sides. I would not be able to stand up, because I need both knees and one hand to stand up. I made a practical decision. I pray I will love this cross of mine more.

That's more than enough about me. I love You and adore You today, and I hope I always will. Teach me to comfort You. I don't care about anything else. You are my love; You are my everything. As you have been telling me, help me to manage my time here at home the way it is managed in the monastery. I must put priorities on things and a time for every needed thing.

Dear love, teach me quickly, please. I am very addicted to materialistic things. With You, my love's help, I am changing to love others.

———— ∽ ————

This Friday, in my mind, I am standing at the foot of Your cross. The sky is dark enough to be night, but when I look up at You, I can see You clearly. I love You, and there is nothing I can do for You. You are so wounded and bloody, it makes me want to cry. I am literally on the verge of tears.

My love, the worst part is that I put You there. You will be with us for only one more hour, and I am already grieving for You. Your mother is here for You, at least, and so is St. John and two holy women. I am sorry, I am sorry, so very sorry. Forgive me.

Now, as I write, I literally do have tears in my eyes. Oh, my poor God. What have I done to You? Now it is hard to see the paper. I had to stop and cry for you. I know that You are really in heaven, and all my meditation on Your crucifixion made me cry.

I called Monsignor, and he kept telling me this was all over. I kept telling him I knew You were really in heaven, but it was my mental meditation that made me cry. I told Monsignor other things, and I stopped crying. I still feel very sorry for what I have done to You, my Lord and my love. Forgive me. Teach me to love You more.

I feel as though a friend or relative has died. I feel as if I am grieving for You and that it is okay to do so, even if You are really in heaven, my love. I think I need to know what it feels like to have You gone. Of course, there was the Resurrection and Ascension.

Thank You, my God, in Your beatific person, for opening up my heart so I could cry for my sins. It's about time, don't You think?

There is so much prayer and other good works that I want to do and so little time. If I live two, five, ten, or twenty years, it is all too little time and suffering for the Kingdom of Heaven. One can never suffer too much, because of our imperfect nature and the sins we continue to commit throughout our life. If all this is joined to Christ's life, His suffering, His Eucharist in the Holy Sacrifice of the Mass said throughout the world, adding His blessed Mother's sinless life and sufferings, then we can do much.

I want to do much for others when I get to heaven, too, just like my friend and my heroine, St. Thérèse of Lisieux. Ideally, in my imagination, she and I will be great friends in heaven. Together, we will take great piles of roses up into bundles in our arms and let them come down to earth for the sake of souls still in the world. Dreams do come true.

My dear love, teach me all You want me to know. Teach me to rejoice in suffering for, through, and with You, my love. Everyone wants to become like the one they love, and I love You. Thank you for giving me Your love. How would I get along without it? You are not the cause of my sufferings but the answer to them.

I think of the ten that You healed. Only one came back to thank You. Your heart was hurt. I thank, adore, worship, and praise You ten times over. I say alleluia ten times over. I love You forever.

Oh, Father, Abba (Daddy), I want to do more than I am doing now. I want to bring throngs of people to You. Use me any way You want. I am all Yours and totally Yours. If You wish, use me in the way we discussed. Use me in an invisible stigmata. Don't let people see me, but You, oh beloved Trinity, in me.

Please keep me very, very humble. I have You and my blessed mother for support. I trust You completely. Thank You, my loves. Again, I feel I must hurry toward You.

Do You know what? I not only love You, but I like You. You are my best friend. You are infinitely forgiving and a good listener. If I could, I would give You so many hugs and kisses. Again, I love You, I trust You, and I thank You.

Dear God, help my friend Monsignor. He had a brilliant mind, but now he is becoming very confused about time and other matters. This must be a terrible cross for him to bear. Thank You, my love, for keeping him humble all these years. His humility will help him get through all that he must in the future. But now he is rapidly going downhill, and he is doing so at an alarming rate.

He has been a spiritual father and friend to me for over thirty years. I pray in great earnestness for him every day now. I think this cross for him could be as humiliating as if someone spit in his face. Being spit upon the face is a cross worse than pain.

The problem with the new pain pills I am on is that I fall asleep more during the day and cannot do all that I need to do. I cannot practice my spiritual discipline as much. This is hard for me. I just want to comfort You, my love, as much as I can. I offer this new cross up to You. I have few answers to this cross, so I will leave the answer up to You. Even so, I thank You for this cross, too. I love, praise, adore, and worship You.

Again, I took one step forward and two steps back. I slept most of the day. I did mourn Jesus, my love, in His dying and death on Good Friday. I was sorry for all the sins I have committed. I felt sorry enough, My Lord, to wish that You had never died for me.

But I want to join You in heaven someday. I know You had to go through Your agony, fourteen stations of Your cross, before Your crucifixion—and the crucifixion itself before anyone could enter heaven. I mourned You at three p.m., the hour of both Your death and the Divine Mercy. I continued to mourn You for a little while.

I called Monsignor to talk about Your death, my Lord. Somehow we got off on the subject of my knees. I didn't call about my sufferings. What I offer up, the pains I have to offer, are like a drop in Your ocean of suffering. If it were not for You, my one-God-in-three-persons, my pain would be unbearable. But with You, my love, I can just bear it. Thank You for helping me in my little cross.

Margaret C. called. At the end of our conversation, she asked if I would like to say a Hail Mary with her. Actually, I wanted to say more prayers than that. So I said, "Why don't we add an Our Father after that?" During these short prayers, I experienced more than a consolation.

Dear God, Margaret C. and I have been talking about doing something for the Blessed Virgin Mary's real birthday, as she calls it. I suggested we split the cost, since I did not have much money. I told Margaret C. we could buy a dozen roses for eighteen dollars at the grocery store. I told her I thought Mary would really like that. Margaret C. said she preferred silk roses or silk flowers. I told her I would leave it up to her.

I carry a new crucifix in my hand wherever I go. This is my signal to God and myself that I am willing to be a victim in any way He chooses. Yes, for You, my love.

Whenever I sin, I ask God to forgive me. However, I don't hurt just God but the whole body of Christ and God. I will continue to ask forgiveness from both during the prayers at the start of Mass.

Canonized saints have carried crosses of heroic proportions. Christ fell on His knees. Saints sometimes fall into sin. If a person on the road to sainthood falls, he or she falls further down. It is no wonder that the soon-to-be canonized think of themselves as the world's greatest sinners.

Jack and I sat down and discussed some aspects of our marriage. We had been living together as brother and sister for years. Even though I think Jack is doing almost perfect work as my husband and caregiver, he said he would try to do better.

When I started to sponsor Margaret, she lived in a town of elderly and orphans where the HIV virus first broke out. The HIV virus killed the parents and made their children orphans. I did not want to spare Margaret anything. In addition to the sponsorship fee, I sent money over for a bed, mattress, sheets, pillows, shoes, underwear, new clothes, private parochial school, uniforms, backpack, atlas, and reams and reams of paper over the years. Jack and I were able to do these things because I sold my diamond bridal ring and gold watch, which cost many thousands of dollars. Of course, we have been helping Margaret for over a decade because we wanted to.

A few years ago, I found out Margaret needed dental work. The sponsorship fee goes far. It covers most of a child's needs, including medicinal needs, but it cannot be stretched far enough to cover dental needs. We asked for an estimate of what Margaret needed in the way of dental work. She needed extensive dental work. We sent the necessary $240 in American money. Over here, the same work would cost thousands of dollars.

While Margaret was having dental work done, and after it was finished, she never complained about anything. She has written us in secret. She says that something is wrong. I haven't been able to find out what is wrong.

To date, Margaret still desires to become a Carmelite nun. She thinks of nothing else. I told Margaret she did not have to become a nun if she did not want to. She said that was not the problem; she still wanted to be a Carmelite. I have told her there are easier orders. Nope. She wants to be a Carmelite. Hurray.

I have just started sponsoring Andy. I asked for a young boy. I hope to offer him the seeds of a vocation, God willing.

Dear one, how will you judge me after I die? The only merits I have, You, my love, have given me. Oh, Holy Trinity, I do trust You. With so many sins on my part, You should have turned me into a pillar of salt long ago. The fact that You have not points clearly to Your unceasing love and compassion and justice, too. Aren't we all born blind due to Satan and original sin?

I would rather die than commit a mortal sin. You, my love, have been hurt down through the ages by everyone. And what can we find that is more sweet, kind, and unceasingly loving than You?

———————⟋⟍⟍———————

I love life. I consider that prayer is my job in life. Couldn't I pray just as well from Purgatory for others? But I know nothing. You are all-love, and with my own stubbornness, I will cling to You now and forever. Because You, my love, will not let anything separate us (Romans 8). Thank You, my adorable one, for being a hound of heaven. In every small, small instance, may I cling to You. Darling, I do love You.

I say I love You; I will become loving. St. Thérèse found her "little way" in scripture. My belief is that by saying "I love You" over and over, I will become heroically loving. I believe, thanks to Margaret C., that I have found my "little way." If I unceasingly tell You I love You, I become, like You, love. Nothing else matters!

And by the way, I love You, love You, love You, love You. Thank You for everything. I have hope. Now I have hope for us being together in heaven sooner. Please say hello to Mother Mary, St. Catherine of Siena, St. Francis, and St. Thérèse. Dearest one, may Your will be done in all things. Amen.

I want to love You as You want me to love You. I want to take my heart and feelings of love out of my heart and give them to You until it is empty. Then I pray that You will fill it up with grace and love again and again and again. I am so thirsty for You, dearest. I beg for Your graces, because I know I am not worthy, and I also know how much You love me. I do trust in You. Please, dear one, fill my mind, heart, and soul. You know what I mean, I know. I am weary.

———————⟋⟍⟍———————

Oh, my beloved one, I am so full of pride. Show me how to be humble. Humility is truth. And You are the truth. I long for You. I want to live as long as I can. I want to serve as long as I can. Yet each new day is one day closer to my goal of union with You, my love, in paradise.

Father Martin asked me why I want to be canonized a saint. The answer is that if God can take me, sinner that I am, and make me a saint, it will give glory to God.

I have been going from one medical problem to another in quick succession. I had two total knee replacements. I got better, but before I was completely well, my kneecap broke when I was coming out of the bathroom. I have had surgery, including a cast and brace. Later on, the cast and brace come off. The physical therapist who came to my home told me that he and my doctor feel I might have to wear a brace on my leg. I worked harder on my exercises. Then he no longer had to help me raise my heel off the bed.

The physical therapist tells me that I won't have to wear a brace. Thank You, my love, for all the graces you gave me to work my hardest on my physical therapy.

I have to force myself to say a rosary along with one that is being said on a religious television show. You and I share something like co-union in silence.

Tomorrow, I will make a conference call with Jack and one of my doctors. In the last two weeks, I have fallen down four times. The people from Med-Act came to get me up off the floor. I think it is no more than low blood pressure. My physical therapist took it this morning, and it was 108 over 48. I love and trust You completely, my God, and my mother, Mary. I love and trust you too.

I have a new ten-year-old, Tony, in Kenya, Africa. Kenya is only one country over from Margaret in Uganda. I have asked for another boy in Kenya. Then Jack and I will have one young lady and three young boys.

I have bought Margaret all the things needed to raise and educate a child in the United States. Hopefully, her decision to become a nun will be fulfilled, and she will help many more people in mind, body, and soul with sacrifice, penance, and other forms of good works like prayer and laughter. Whatever Margaret becomes, by Your grace, Jack and I have, and are, doing good works for her in every way. Thank You, my loving and great God, for the opportunity and grace to help her.

The tables could be turned. Margaret could be helping Jack and I. When we give Margaret good works, it is, like I have said, like throwing pebbles into a pond and watching the rippling effect upon the water. Eventually, the rippling water becomes rushing water of good works and grace given by You in the first place.

The young men I sponsor in Kenya are Amos, Andy, and Frank. They sometimes need to fight famine in Kenya. Too often, the people of Kenya plant their crops only to see them scorched by the sun when the rain that came does not stay long enough. Despite this, Amos wrote to me that we should not spend the whole twenty-five-dollar sponsorship fee on himself and his family. He said that he had enough of everything and Jack and I might need a little of the money back. He surely found a place in my heart. He will make a wonderful addition to the priesthood or any other vocation, because in spite of his poverty, he knows how to give and to love.

Margaret became a Catholic after I started sponsoring her through the project foundation. I know Satan does not want bush children to become Catholic nuns, priests, and married family people. I am not as smart as Satan, but I know I can be brave with

You as my love. Everyone in heaven helps me. I know You always will. Pray for me, Mother, St. Michael, all you angels and saints.

———∞———

I am trying to do Your will as I see it, my dear, dear love. All good, all love, all God.

I am exercising every day for an hour of vigorous exercise to bring my knee back to where it was before I broke the kneecap. It looks like now I may have to wear a big brace. And I have exercised vigorously because that is the way I exercise. But also, so I won't have to wear a leg brace. A leg brace is nothing; its restrictions are nothing. Compared to Your agony, I will rejoice in a leg brace. Thank You, my love.

———∞———

Oh, my love, when You look down at me, I hope You see me and say, "Yes, there is my servant Mary Faith, who is willing to do anything to serve Me." I am willing, Lord, but so weak. But that does not diminish Your merciful love for and to me. Let me always be willing to do what Your will is for me.

In Your infinite mercy, You love me. Attract me to Your infinite love. Thank You, my love, with all my heart, mind, and strength. Watch over me lest I fall into sin. Show me more and more the reality of my love and the reality of my sinfulness. I love, praise, and adore You, my all-gracious God.

———∞———

I pray the rosary and the descent of the Holy Spirit upon the apostles and Mary in the form of tongues of fire over each head. Mary was conceived immaculately, and she received the

Holy Spirit when He came to her when Jesus was conceived. Yet Mary also received a tongue of fire on her head when the apostles did. Why she would need to receive the Holy Spirit twice is a mystery to me.

The angels are all more intelligent than we are, the guardian angels being the least intelligent. St. Michael is the most intelligent being, the highest angel. Yet a mere mortal, Mary, is the Queen of Heaven and his queen, because she always said yes to God.

Why on earth did Satan, who was higher than St. Michael, want to become like God? He had it all. Now he has nothing and never will have God again. This scares me to death. Lord, If I am not humble, make me humble. And if I am humble, please give me the grace to become more and more humble each moment, each day. And if I am completely full of worldliness, as I think I am, humble me.

———$\sim$———

Oh, my good Savior, Your words "I thirst" run throughout my mind over and over. You were given vinegar to ease Your all-consuming thirst. Before Your crucifixion, Roman guards mocked Your divine kingship by whipping You, Jesus, forty-one times; crowning You, my God, with a crown of thorns; and spitting in Your face. When they spit in Your face, it was worse than another beating, because such an act is so demoralizing. You, my love, took all this, the way of the cross, and the crucifixion for every one of us, sinners all. You are pure love, and I discover this more and more each day.

Be with me so I may love You and adore You in awe. Christ, You are the Source of all grace. Thank You, my love, for suffering for me. You, Lord, have given grace to my heart. My heart wants to beat in unison with Yours. Teach me that this may be.

Even if my heart is pierced by excruciating love, I desire You fervently. Everything must come from You, my love. I can undergo anything to be united to You. Jesus, I trust in You to make all things good. If I simply hold my hand out for You to hold, nothing can separate us. I love You. I love You over and over again. You are my precious God of love and adoration.

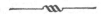

Lord, I have sinned against You. I have fallen into sin while proclaiming my love for You. Most Holy God, I know of the warmth of Your love as it washes over me, sinner that I am. Help me to keep saying I love You. I want to run to You and not away. Love me. Make me humble of heart as only You can do. I am made in the image of You, which is love itself.

Help me to run the race quickly, for I feel I must run quickly. Help me give all of myself to You, my love, and others. I have a few years to run with my cross. In the blink of an eye, I will be seventy or eighty years old, if I am lucky.

May I receive more and more of Your body and blood. I do want to love You. I am trying. I love You for all that You are to me. I love You. I love You. But I do not love You enough yet. I want my soul to grow. Jesus, I do trust in You.

In elementary school, the other children teased me often. There were many good things that happened to me when I was young too. I was talking to a longtime friend on the phone long-distance last night and remembered the point in time in school when I decided I would be good to others from then on, because I knew how the ordeals I was going through hurt.

I hope and pray earnestly, Lord, that I am walking the walk

and talking the talk to sainthood. If I am not, my love, please show me my own self-deceit and disguise. The only thing I really want is You, my Trinity, and heaven.

Our hearts are locked in prayer again. Oh, sweet love, I will be Your victim and Your stigmatic. I will give my life for You. I will do anything. Just grant me the strength of grace. Vincent said he would never deny You, and he did. Please, my adorable one, my all good one, help me, because if Vincent could deny You, so can I. Just give me grace, humility, and overflowing love and zeal for You. Oh, dearest God and Savior, I love You. I love You. I do not tire of saying it. I love You, and I want to say it throughout eternity.

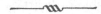

Lord, lead me forward in Your Grace. I want real holiness. Psalm 25 says, "Remember that your compassion, O Lord, and your kindness are from old. The sins of my youth and my frailties remember not; in your kindness remember me because of your goodness O Lord." I thank You over and over for converting me from a suffering agnostic—for sending Mary to me, which made me search out membership in Your holy Roman Catholic and Apostolic Church.

I thank You for keeping me in a state of grace now. There is no way in this lifetime that I can thank You enough, my love. I hope to be able to express my undying gratitude in heaven throughout eternity.

Oh, dearest one, have I ever told You that I love You? No? Well, let me tell You. I know, my love, my Trinity, that I love You and want to love You and my neighbor in whom You are until my heart breaks of love.

Recently, I went to the doctor's office. He has done ten surgeries on me in about two to three years. I am on the painkiller morphine He told me my last surgery was unsuccessful and I would need to wear a leg brace and use a walker the rest of my life. He said that he could try again, but if my knee was infected, I could only live in a wheelchair for the rest of my life.

I knew the operation was unsuccessful before he told me. Since the operation, I have been working at rigorous physical therapy with all my heart and soul for an hour a day. My legs were strong, but my knee responded only a little after months of this exercise. The doctor said good results on a second surgery were only fifty-fifty.

I eat, rest, pray, and watch television in a lift chair. Because I have a torn rotator cuff in my right shoulder, I cannot get comfortable in bed, so I sleep in the lift chair too. My walker and commode are three feet from the lift chair. I live in a five-by-five-foot space, but living this way is only temporary. Jack has promised to purchase a bed I can sleep in comfortably.

Mother Mary has promised heaven to any devoted to her rosary. I love you. Pray for us all my great, great love. I worship You, my God, and I thank You for taking my cross and giving me resurrection.

I did not say the three rosaries I promised yesterday. I started coughing and could not stop. I had my emergency inhaler. Accidentally, I fell asleep. Yesterday, I went to a different type of doctor, and it wore me out. That is why I fell asleep.

I have had so many health problems in life recently. I tried to ignore it when I felt pain in my chest. A doctor diagnosed asthma, bronchitis, and a bladder infection after eight hours in the emergency room of a hospital.

I am in love with You even when I am hurting. I love You

and Mary, my mother and other love. Someday, I will be happy in heaven. I am looking forward to seeing You, my Father, Son, and Holy Spirit. I love You, my adorable one-God-in-three-persons. I stand in the light of the cross and rejoice. Oh joy, I have another chance to offer all to God and Mary.

One thing I really like about the morning offering and this great church of ours is that we can offer up our joys as well as the sufferings, prayers, works, and sorrows, disappointments and frustrations. On a Catholic religious show on the television, I saw the quotation, "One just soul can save thousands of sinners." As God leads me to become just, this is my mission.

On every matter, I want to imitate the saints and try to do the heroically virtuous thing. Holy Spirit, show me the truth over the next month about what I should do about my last operation. Every day, I pray about this. Perhaps I am giving this more importance than it is due.

Dearest love, make me a saint for Your greater glory. More than anything, keep me humble. Humility is honesty and truth. Let me be honest about my sinful, fallen nature. Allow me to run after the truth. Dear, dear Jesus, let me run after You.

Margaret has complained that the girls were mean to her. I told her they were naturally jealous of her. We had arranged to send twenty dollars a month to the foundation and fifteen dollars a month directly to her indefinitely. In December, we sent her forty-five dollars. Thirty of that was for her, and I explained she should do good to her enemies, these jealous girls. I asked her to go to each girl and ask what she would like to have.

I think I was asking too much of a nineteen-year-old. She told Father John that she was going to visit relatives for a week. She has a brother in the seminary. I am afraid she has taken the money I sent her and run away. I am praying and praying for her. Perhaps she felt I did not understand her.

Mother Mary, I know a little about how you and St. Joseph felt when you could not find Jesus. I just wanted to love her and give her everything she needed. My dear love, I know she is Your child more than mine and you, Mother Mary, the angels and saints will watch over her. I am sorry if I have not been a good mother to her despite the best intentions.

The next two days, I was calm, very calm, because I knew God, Mary, and her guardian angel would protect her. I called Father John again, and he laughed and told me he had confused Margaret with another girl. Margaret was in school where she was supposed to be. I had asked him to call me collect anytime day or night when he found out about Margaret, and he did not. I was mad, but I forgave him.

For the first two days when I thought she was gone, I was upset because I thought she was running around with forty-five dollars in American money. I told Father John cashiers in convenience stores here sometimes are robbed in the store for that amount of money and occasionally the robbers kill the cashier. Perhaps he laughed out of embarrassment. I am sorry I made him uncomfortable. I wished he had called me, though, when he found out that Margaret was fine.

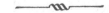

My God, please help me to grow in grace that I might become a victim soul for You, my love, and all for Your greater glory. Not my will, but Yours, my God, be done. I am determined to reach heaven someday. It will be all by Your love and grace. Please, please keep me humble. The reason I want to use my sufferings is for Your greater glory, primarily, and secondarily, for the reparation of my many sins, the healing of bodies, and the salvation of souls.

This is what I mean when I say I want to be a victim soul. I believe other people might have a different definition of what it means to be a victim soul. As I have said before, I do not believe that God, who is all good, will cause harm or cause a soul to be victimized.

A friend of mine who I have known for thirty-seven years cannot understand the fact that I will use my sufferings joyously for the health of others. To my good friend, this is not right. I consider prayer to be my vocation in life. She stands by the scripture that says, "By His stripes we are healed." She very regularly prays this prayer for herself and expects God to heal her. She only wants what she lovingly thinks is the best for me.

She says she cannot find any reference in scripture for what I am trying to do. However, God did tell us to take up our cross and follow Him. The church teaches that we should all try to imitate the saints in heroic virtue. I am trying to stay very near the foot of the cross with Mary, the cross of Jesus crucified. Thank You, my love for the grace and light to do this. Don't let me stand just at the foot of Your crucifixion but become part of it, that I might decrease and You increase.

Again, I have in my mind an image of Your crucifixion. The sky is black, but everything can be clearly seen. Mary and John are there. The other two Marys are there, and I am standing at the foot of the cross. One of the two Marys is Mary Magdalene. I don't know who the other is. Perhaps she is Lazarus's sister. This is the image in my mind of the crucifixion.

Sometimes when I think that it is my sins that crucified You, my love, I literally cry. It is very hard for me to say the sorrowful mysteries of the rosary and think that the one I love above all

others was made to suffer so brutally by men. You came to redeem
and love. I thank You ten times over for loving me. I remember
the time, my dearest one, when You healed ten and only one came
back to thank You. I know Your feelings were hurt.

St. Thérèse of Lisieux said that it was God who placed in her
heart the desire to be a saint and that He would not have done it
if it was impossible. I hope the same holds true for me.

It has been a dry month. Thank You, dearest love, for the
Communion a while ago. Today I asked for You to come, and
You did indeed. You told me we can be one even as I am doing
other tasks. Until tonight it was prayer, tasks, or Communion. I
now know all can come in the same moment in time. Cross or
glory—I just want to be next to You. Oh, my good love, I thank
You for this gift. Help me to love You forevermore.

Teach and lead me like a child. You have left a mark on my
soul tonight. It's the middle of the night, and I want to go outside
and shout for joy to anyone around. How can anyone refuse Your
delicate love and Your strongest love? Alleluia!

I just prayed to my mother Mary for my natural mother and
father and my ancestors. My ancestors came to this country to
escape Catholicism.

I talked to Monsignor today, and he said he is going to have to
sell his car. He and I are both going to have to get used to the idea
of not driving again. I am resolved not to upset Monsignor with
my problems, but to let him tell me his. He has been my spiritual
father since I first met him thirty-two-years ago. I remember
meeting him as if it was yesterday.

We have a purely spiritual love for one another. Just a few moments ago, I prayed to Mary to ask the Father, her Son, and the Holy Spirit to restore his hearing and some of the memories he has lost. He talks openly to me about his problems. I am very happy he feels he can do this. I feel that in some manner, our places have switched. How happy I am to have a chance to listen to him. I want to help him in the aging process in every possible way.

In praying for a miracle for Monsignor, perhaps I am not being practical. But miracles happen, and they are never practical. I love him spiritually. My love, please grant him many graces. You and Mary will always be my first loves, and my love throughout all eternity, whenever that begins for me. Once again I love and worship You. May this grow in me.

Father Martin is coming today to hear my confession, anoint me, and give me Communion. I am going to prepare for his coming and consider my sins to make a good confession. I love You. Thank you, my Lady, for all Your prayers and intercessions for me and those I love.

Oh, dear love, You have suffered for and because of me. Let me know suffering for You, with the inspiration of Your love and grace. It is not suffering for suffering's sake, but suffering already present, offered freely to You for all those I know, including my pastor (spiritual director) and my parish. I also pray for all who have been, those here now, and those babies not born yet. I want to pray especially for children of every time and age. I could not offer any sufferings or prayers without Your all-loving grace that You, dearest love, have given me first.

People tell me I am changing. Margaret C. says I seem more mature and calm. I do feel calm. It is Your Loving presence that makes me calm.

A friend from college has said my complexion seems clearer. I have not done anything to my face. Some of the priests and participants in the Mass on the Catholic television network seem to glow with the holiness of Christ in their faces. I am not saying this is happening to me. How wonderful it would be if people could look at others and see the good and not the bad.

I have some pictures in the living room of Jack and me. One picture was taken fifteen or twenty years ago. Someone said I look younger now than in that picture. My love, You told us to let our light to shine among men. I ardently hope You are shining through me. I love You.

When I look at my sins, I feel a loathing. I never can understand how I can treat You, my adorable one, so badly. St. Paul said that he did not do the good he wanted to do. He also said that he did the bad that he did not want to do.

Jack just went to bed. We watched a Catholic program on television called *The Journey Home*. While watching this show, I was seized with emotion, I suppose, and cried out to Jack how I try to pray every day that he will become a Roman Catholic. I also pray that he will become a canonized saint. I offer the sufferings I am feeling now for this purpose.

Oh, my love, just let me do Your will. Before I can become a saint, I must grow closer and closer to You until we are one and people. Don't look at Mary Faith and see Mary Faith but Father, Christ, and Holy Spirit in one Holy Trinity. My one-in-three, my one-love-in-three-persons, I am confident in You.

It's not that I want to become big like You, but ever smaller and more like You. I need all Your help in my sinfulness and trials. Oh, the Holy Trinity comes close. Thank You for all the favors You have and are continuing to give me, my love. All things do and will work to the good for those who love God.

I turned the television on and saw the body and blood of Christ being elevated. I adored Christ until the end of Mass, and when He was shown after Mass in the monstrance.

It dawned on me that with the electric wheelchair a salesperson showed me, I could take myself to Mass seven days a week, since the church is only two blocks away. Oh, what a joy that would be. I am leaving it in Your hands and your hands, my lady and mother. Mary, if this comes about, I will try to get the kind with a color choice, and in your honor I will choose blue.

I love You, Lord, and I just want to be loved by You and Mary forever. I have suffered very little in my life. You told us to take our cross and follow You. If some people would know my life story, these people might say I have suffered much. But my life has never been on the line. I pray to You, my love, that good or bad, whatever life holds for me, I will always choose you and heaven. I am determined to reach You in heaven someday. I know, my love, You are more determined for me to be in heaven than I am.

Lord, let me be unselfish in my relationships with You and everyone else. Please give me the grace to move ever forward and freely surrender my will to Yours. Oh, my love, in every moment of every day, let me commune with You while I do everything else. Let every moment be a time of saying yes to Your all-loving will.

As a small child, and as I was growing up, my family provided many forms of delight. However, I experienced many forms of abuse as I grew up as well. The children in my classes at school taunted me at every opportunity. These children attended church where my family did. I remember the very day that I said to myself, "If this is Christianity, then I want no part of it."

In high school, I remember telling the biology teacher that if there was a God, I didn't know how He could let such suffering happen in the world. I now know I did not see how He could let so much suffering go on in my life.

In college, students were required to attend a chapel service every Wednesday. I was supposed to be a Protestant and disliked every minute of the Protestant service, as I recall. Then I found out I could attend the Catholic service, which consisted of the Catholic priest coming and talking to the students. I was delighted to hear that he only came from another college half the time. We could sign a piece of paper and leave if he was ten minutes late. When he did not show up, I had fifty minutes of free time, which I spent in the college coffeehouse drinking coffee, smoking, and having a good time. I gloated that I was out of the Protestant service. Dear one, forgive me.

In my sophomore year, the head of the English department, who was my student advisor, convinced me to take a course on religion. It was a Protestant course, because my parents sent me to a Protestant college. I made a 360-degree turn and zealously wanted to become Catholic. Both my parents threw a fit.

In obedience to my parents, I waited until after I graduated from college. They thought it was a whim. I was conditionally rebaptized on November 16, 1968. The night, before I left for baptism, my mother threw a crucifix and a rosary at me. My dad was upset, hurt, and angry.

I thank you, my God, and Mary for turning me around. I

love You, my God of mercy, for saving my soul. I have become someone who will do anything for Your love and who wants to try, with the grace and mercy You have given me, to become a saint. I thank You now, and I hope to thank You through all eternity.

———————ᘜᘜ———————

I broke my right heel in three places and also the ankle on both sides. The doctors all got together to decide what to do with me. They decided not to do surgery and put pins in, because they were afraid the leg might become infected and eventually need to be amputated. The doctors decided to put my leg in a cast and leave it on an extra-long time. It needed to be on for three or four months.

After the cast was put on, I was in a nursing home for three to four weeks. The charge nurse was mean. Carl always had a smile on. God bless Carl. An aide was mean. I told her I was going to leave the nursing home. She began a litany of all the reasons I could not do that.

That day, I saw my doctor, and I came back to the aide with a slip from him releasing me to go home that day. Then the aide could not have been nicer. "Let me get your shoes. Let me help you with that," etc. The mean charge nurse gave me a hug before going home. I guess they were afraid I was going to sue them. I did not.

After I got home, I first learned to stand up and turn to use my walker to go from one room to another. Lynn helped me personally and cleaned everything in sight. She moved to Arkansas after about four weeks. I gave her a scapular medal, and she took another for a grandson she thought needed it.

She was replaced by a young lady named Jane who deep-cleaned everything in sight. She practically worked herself out of work. She cleaned everything thoroughly. She will start cleaning the walls tomorrow. I am adding money to the money she usually makes from an agency. We have fun and enjoy each other.

Lynn and Jane are just the opposite of the people in the nursing home. Thank You, my love, for sending them to me. Each has been a great blessing. I thank You ten times over, my love.

One day, all I could think of was the things my walker was keeping me from doing. Tearfully, I called Monsignor. When my cuckoo clock struck six times, he said, "Those darned birds. I am going to come down there with my gun and shoot every one of them. Their feathers will be flying. And after I shoot them, I am going to bury them." I started to roar with laughter. I couldn't stop laughing. Monsignor is such a wonderful priest.

The next morning, I no longer thought of my walker as a ball and chain but as a means of transportation. I called Monsignor again and asked if he had been praying for me. He said he had. I thought he might be responsible for my change of outlook. God bless Monsignor. When I pray, I always pray for Monsignor.

Oh, my God, where are You? I can't seem to find You, not even in Communion. When I receive You, my beloved, I feel nothing at all. In whatever state I find myself, I promise to give you all my love.

Margaret C. said that I am walking, perhaps, through the desert. Help me, my love. May Your glorious will be done. Sacred heart of Jesus and the immaculate heart of Mary, I consecrate myself to You, as I try to do each day. Take my heart, sacred heart of Jesus, and put it into a hidden niche of Your heart, which is an ocean of love. Keep me hidden in this niche that I may be Yours forever. Dearest one, throughout my life, keep me humble, that I can truly be united to You, my adorable love.

Jane left for a job working with the mentally challenged. She will be coming back every other week to clean. I am looking forward to her coming back, even if it is for only one day every two weeks.

Jennifer took over after Jane. She was different from Jane in cleaning and has what seems like a chip on her shoulder. I told her she tries to act tough but isn't inside. When I looked at her, I saw a hurt little girl.

She told me about her experience with her mother, her mother's husband, and the other patients around. She has had to be off work at least once because of an encounter with her patient. Friday she sat cross-legged on the bed with me and petted Lady Regina. It is a small success. She let her defenses down.

Friday, I was in pain. I have said that with God's power, He could squash us like bugs for offending Him. Friday, the devil said to me, "What do you think he is doing now?" I felt like a squashed bug, but I realized that the devil and original sin did it. Thank You, Lord, for helping me get through Friday.

Oh, author of all love, I love You and want to love You more and more each day. I adore You, worship You, and praise You over and over. The situation demands it. Without Your infinite love, I could have lost You forever and won, if one could call it winning, the devil and hell.

Thank You for allowing me to see that I needed to pray more for my brother and my whole extended family. My sister-in-law says the prayers are starting to work. Of course, it is You working through me. Keep me humble, please, Lord.

My God, I want to be with You; our Lady, my mother; and all the angels and saints. Mostly, I want to be with You. I am not depressed. I want to come home. I cannot think of coming home. Much in the way of prayers need to be said first. Also, somehow, in the short period of time allotted to me, I must receive sanctity from You.

I feel almost abandoned by God and almost without hope for heaven. I told this to Margaret C., and she said again that I was probably walking in a desert without consolation. That is certainly the truth. I asked her to pray for me. She asked me to pray for her in a particular regard. I need Your help most of all, my God: Father, Son, and Holy Spirit. You are my loves in trinity.

I know that feelings of abandonment can be very good or the occasion of sin. I sometimes feel that I sin against You, but without my consent, making this perhaps no sin at all? I have been struggling with this for years. The part about feeling almost abandoned and without hope is new. May you, my Lady, and all in heaven pray for me. I love you, my Lady of Perpetual Help. Help me, my beautiful love and spiritual bridegroom. I do love You, even if I cannot feel it or feel being loved.

I am worried somewhat about Margaret C. She had a cancerous growth removed from her nose. She told me she has a shadow on one lung. I pray that the cancer has not spread. Please, my love, let me help Margaret C. in this matter, whether it be by prayer for the miraculous or penance for the same. I would not wish cancer on my worst enemy, let alone on this good friend of mine who brings me You three times a week. May I be obedient to Your will, O my beloved, as I pray and do penance for Margaret C.

————※————

The hope for heaven that I do have comes from Your grace, which tells me, O my beloved, that You are infinitely good, just, loving, and merciful. Without this grace, I would feel totally abandoned and without hope for heaven. As it is, I see the light of merciful love at the end of the tunnel.

I am tired, but I praise You, adore You, worship You, thank You, love You many, many times over. In doing this, I may not feel loved, but know that I am. Sacred heart of Jesus and the immaculate heart of Mary, I always want to consecrate myself to You, my love, my great love, and you, my queen of heaven, every day. Jesus, I trust in You.

But please, I implore You, keep me humble or humiliate me that I will not be truly be abandoned by You and lose heaven. Detach me from my overattachment to the world and worldly things. As You have said to me many times, everything outside of You is nothingness.

Oh, Holy Mother of God, Mary, keep me and watch over me as I try to walk toward our Father, your Son, and your spouse, the Holy Spirit, my one-God-in-three-persons, all of which I adore, all of which give me graces to adore and every good thing.

I have been experiencing a little of this darkness recently. But all things are well, just as all things work together for good for those who love God. In darkness or in light, I want to love You, but this darkness is new to our love. Help me to find and praise You in the dark. Keep me silently looking for You each day, looking in the dark.

————※————

Good morning, my love. I offer You my prayers, works, joys, sufferings, sorrows, disappointments, and frustrations. I consecrate myself to your sacred heart and the immaculate heart of Mary, my mother. I do this in union with the Masses said throughout the world and for the pope's intentions.

I pray for Margaret in Uganda and for my three boys in Kenya. I pray for the pope in mind, heart, body, and soul. I pray for whatever You want and for everyone on my long list of prayers. I pray for priests, religious, deacons, communion ministers, the people in my parish, and my pastor, who is my spiritual director. I also pray for Monsignor's hearing and mental acuity; the conversion of my husband, Jack, to the Roman Catholic Church; and the Carmelite sisters' needs. I love You. I hope that what I do today will be pleasing to You, my love. Thank You for loving me so much.

When I look at all the hard things I have had to endure, I say that to me, these are my greatest joys, because I have something to offer to You, my beloved. And as I look back at my life, I see the times You have unfolded me in Your protective hands. How can I begin to adore, worship, thank, praise, or love You enough? I will spend my eternity doing so, in loving awe of Your beatific vision.

I offered something to You. I know You are an almighty God with an exquisitely strong desire and infinite ability to help us in every respect. When I offer anything to You, my love, I am confident in You, and I trust You. My love, I am waiting to see Your face. Oh, what a happy day.

You and I know we love one another. I ask pardon every time I need it. I wish we had enough priests so I could go to the Sacrament of Reconciliation once a week. I used to. I miss it and need it. You seem so far away, and I just don't know why I feel this way. Is it through my faults? I only want to love You with my whole heart, mind, soul, being, and every breath I take. I used to be so at peace, and now I wonder why I am distracted.

The fire department said to me I need to live in assisted living. I keep falling down. Sometimes I break bones. I need to pray about this. Even so, I adore, worship, praise, thank, love, and sing to You, my dearest love.

I am made in the likeness and image of God. But my God, I cannot find You. All is well. Wherever You lead, I will follow. I am so sorry for the sins I have committed against You, my God, and against Mary, for her heart was pierced seven times. Lift me up into Your arms and out of the mire of my sins.

I feel so sorry for You, Jesus. I am very sorry for what I did to You. Please, God and Mary, forgive me. I do know I love You, even if I cannot see or feel Your presence.

All I need to do is take up my cross daily without worry and put myself lovingly in a lower position of service to the world and those in purgatory. Thank You for showing me this, O dear love. I must only stay in the present moment of love. This has been a banner day. Thank You, my love and holy one. Things are better now. I am in love with You. It is the anniversary of my conditional baptism.

Please help me, Lord. I keep trying to spend more time with You and less time with worldly things. I try to do what You are calling me to do. But it is one step forward and two steps back sometimes. Please give me the grace I need to do better. Ask for grace, and you will receive it. Seek grace, and you'll find it. I am asking and seeking grace, my good love. You are grace.

Seek first the kingdom and its righteousness. All the rest will be given to everyone. Thank You for the church, tradition, the Bible; the mystical body of Christ; our Blessed Mother, Mary; the angels and saints; and the pope. Of course, I thank You for Your body and blood, the Holy Sacrifice of the Mass, the Sacraments, the Divine Mercy and its chaplet, and the Holy Rosary. I adore, worship, praise, and love You. I want to thank You—now and throughout all eternity.

Make me holy, O my good Lord. You are the great love of my life. Of course I love Jack, but You are God. I offer myself to You each day in mind, body, and soul. I love You with a ferocity, and I am running toward You.

Nevertheless, this Lent has not been the one of last year. Last year, I did not run, I flew. You carried me high as I said three or four rosaries a day and was glued to the Catholic television network. I prayed quietly to You. My prayer was more peaceful then. Let me fly again, Lord. I just want to be holy, as You want me to be holy. I am nowhere near the saint You want all of us to become. I trust in You for this and everything else.

To me, reality (You) seems so white and bright. It sparkles everywhere. Two of my friends have cut their arms enough to leave scars on their forearms. One is the most loving, giving person you would want to meet. But she described her reality to me as very dark and with two round white circles and a number two. I feel for her greatly. She says she is all right now. But she told me she lied to her psychiatrist on how well she felt to get out of the mental hospital.

I have been praying for her while I write. I am still learning how to pray constantly. I find myself in prayer to You, no matter what I am doing. I am only learning. I do not do this all the time. I feel a little abashed now if I don't have anything to offer you.

———— ⚬⚬⚬ ————

Right now, I have had a total of twenty-two surgeries. I have a few diseases, one of which keep me from going to Mass and adoration chapel. One time the fragrance of the candles in the adoration chapel started to make me feel as though my chest was closing, and I had to leave. That is something I really want to do; adore You in Your monstrance. Oh well, the next time I can get to church, I will go into the sanctuary. The candles are less per square inch of air there.

I am very grateful for the tabernacle. But it is not face to face as You are to me when You are in a monstrance.

———— ⚬⚬⚬ ————

Jack and I could not have children, and he did not want to adopt. I felt I should help at least one child in the world. I asked a global foundation for their neediest girl. I thought I would have more empathy for a girl rather than a boy at that time.

The global foundation gave me Margaret, who was the neediest child in the world. I promised myself that I would do more than sponsor her for a low fee each month. I promised myself I would raise her like my own American daughter.

Jack and I have been giving the sponsor fee and adding to it since Margaret was eleven. Her parents died of AIDS. She came from the bush country of Uganda. She could not read or write her own language.

Jack and I entered Margaret into a private parochial school. Over the years, she always had new clothes and anything and everything to help her in her schoolwork. Margaret always worked very, very hard at her studies, and she did excellent work.

Now she is twenty-five. Margaret reads, writes, speaks, and thinks in English. She is now in her second year at a Uganda university and is majoring in teaching and education. She began doing her own good works years ago when she joined the AIDS Youth Challenge and warned young people about the ongoing problem of AIDS. She also worked on her parish liturgy.

Now her pebbles of good are becoming rushing water (grace). They will ripple and rush the water a thousand times over when she is teaching. I will shortly include my letters to Margaret and hers to me.

For several years, Jack and I have also been sponsoring three boys in Kenya. All three of them are growing into fine young men. All three know each other. We no longer have the money to do more than give the requested sponsor fee for each of these teenagers. They face famine. I am told when they plant crops, they get some rain, but not enough to keep the sun from scorching their crops. The global foundation makes sure the children are fed, clothed, attend school, and receive any necessary medicinal needs.

For these poor little boys and girls, my children tell me, entering into this global foundation, the Christian Foundation for Children and Aging, is like a dream come true. One of my young men told me that he had too much and we need not send in the full sponsorship amount if we needed it more than he did. Can you imagine this? He is not a young man, a teenager, but fully a man with a heart of love.

Ask yourself if you can give good works here and there. Or

would you be able to give a little to a global foundation like the foundation? It has its global headquarters in Kansas City, Kansas. The telephone number is 800-875-6564. I have seen the pebbles of my good works ripple the water and watched the ripples grow larger and larger.

I chose the foundation because I could give to poor little children and watch their lives change for the better. You might want to make your difference, your mark that you were here, by helping the crippled boy down the street or the aging senior next door. Give what you can give, no matter how small or large. God will smile upon you and be so proud of you for your own pebbles of good works.

You will leave an indelible mark on the recipient of your work. God will mark you indelibly as *very good* forever. God has a long memory about good works and who does them. He has a very short memory about sins confessed. You can make your mark wherever forever.

I have been watching Mass on television, unable to get to church for years. Very recently, I found out about the county wheelchair bus and have gone to Mass twice in the last two weeks on it. That's as often as I could attend Mass due to the bus service's busy schedule, which is mainly for medical assistance.

I have found a wheelchair van that will get me to church for Mass as often as I want. Thank You, Lord, for all the graces You have given me. Thank You, my God, for my wheelchair van. It is glorious. Everything you do makes me love You more.

What a glory-filled day. Sitting outside the church after Mass, I looked at the scenery of lacy green leaves, two large brilliant evergreens, and the blue sky. All I could see was a wonder of wonders. Nature said "God" on every tree and evergreen, and in the sky. I wish everyone would stop and look, and then come inside our great church. May God give this grace to everyone.

———∽∞∽———

The Catholic television had the singer Dennis McNeil on. He sang with his excellent, opera-trained voice. He sang three songs that pulled at the heartstrings. They were "Ave Maria," "Danny Boy," and "How Great Thou Art." I hope to get some of his music sometime soon. Tiny tears of joy.

———∽∞∽———

Thank You for revealing to me that I should trust You more in intercessory prayer. You know before I do what I want to ask of You. I am afraid I stand guilty of nagging You. There is an ocean of difference between a litany and a nag. And You are all love and all-knowing.

You are the opposite of the unjust judge who finally gave in to the widow so she would go away and leave him alone. You are more than happy to answer my silly whims if they are innocent and free of any wrongdoing. My love, I will feel free to ask but not to nag. Thank You for showing me how to trust You more and more every day.

———∽∞∽———

My cross is so small compared to Yours, my God. It is an honor and a joy to stand on a cross next to You. I know that with my physical problems, suffering is bound to come. Suffering comes, I believe in my instance, from my having been born two months premature. I have had twenty-two operations, including osteoarthritis, fibromyalgia, diabetes, cold asthmatic attacks, and COPD. I forgot to mention that I am crippled and have bladder and bowel problems.

God is not giving me these problems. I was born two months premature. That is one reason I have so many physical problems. However, the reason behind my premature birth is Satan and original sin. I want to remain true to God, my love, and fight my physical maladies. I go to doctors and take morphine-based medicine, but I cannot take enough to make the pain go away. When I have taken a prescribed dose, I itch from my scalp down. Thus I am able to offer my sufferings to God.

God's people will be helped from what I suffer and offer up to our Father with Christ. When I stand on the cross, I am closest to Christ crucified. I am very happy to be needed. Even when I am suffering, I am happy. And every day, I ask him to take my suffering for the souls in purgatory, the souls here now, the dying souls especially, and for the babies' souls in each mother's womb. In this way, I give my will to God.

Years ago, I was afraid to suffer. God has given me the grace of joy. I am sure he will reward me even more now and in heaven. As Pope John Paul the great said, "Do not be afraid." I love you, Lord. I do love you, my God.

———✺———

Oh, Lord, the slightest expression of love on my part brings down an ocean of love on Your part. I adore You, worship You, thank You, praise You, and most of all, love You. I ask pardon for those who do not adore You, worship You, thank You, praise You, or love You. This is the Fatima prayer, and it has become a litany for me. I say it whenever I glorify Your will, O Lord, even when it is not mine. Praise God for giving me this grace.

Even if Your will is not what I would choose, I rejoice in

doing it. You are all good, and so is Your will. Thank You, my God and love, for now and forevermore. Someday I will be in heaven where I can adore You and sing praises of Your glory through all eternity. I praise You now, while doing other things, because of Your magnificent goodness to me. I know only goodness and love come from You. I desire to abandon my will to Yours in utter trust.

I wish there was the highest mountain in the world, and it had an echo that could be heard all over the world. I would want to be on that mountain, and I would shout in echo, "God is love, and *He loves you.*"

Oh, my good and gracious God, I want to follow Your will for me absolutely. I do not believe there is any part that does not want Your present and future will. I want Your will with my mind, heart, strength, and soul. Thank You for giving me this grace along with a shower of graces You have already given me. "I have been rejoicing each day in Your will. Your will is my greatest good, because you are all love."

I look out my window on a day like today, when the sky is bright blue and the trees' leaves are enlightened along with shrubs to a brilliant, outstanding green by the sun, and I can only say thank You. I pray for the people who have asked me to pray for them or for their relatives. I am usually asked to pray for those who have cancer. I also pray for a friend's grandson who has spina bifida and scoliosis—if, O Lord, he could only run and play with the other young people his age. May Your great, loving, and majestic will be done for all these.

Thank You for the cancer cures, my love. You cured them; I only prayed and offered up my sufferings at that time. I am the wood, and You are the divine fire. Without the divine fire, all that is there is a bunch of sticks. Thank you, my love. Although the little boy has not been cured physically, he has only a very little time with his grandmother, because he says he is having too much fun playing with classmates at school. May God bless everyone who reads this book, now and forever.

Mary Faith

LETTERS AND EMAILS

$\mathcal{N}$ow I would like to turn to some of the letters and emails Margaret and I wrote each other.

Letters

1996

May 1996

Dear Sponsor,

I am a translator and friend of your sponsored child Margaret. Little Margaret is only 11 years old and does not read or write yet. Margaret will be happy to have you for her new friend. Margaret lives in the country of Uganda. Here many people grow coffee as a chief crop. Our country is a little poor but people are very good and work hard. I hope you will write to Margaret, and you become good friends.

May God bless you

September 24, 1996

Dearest Margaret,

I liked your picture in your school uniform. I hoped you liked your birthday presents. Margaret, the Claddagh ring (pronounced *Clad da*) is a sign of many things. The hands clasped together mean friendship. The heart above means love, and the crown stands for loyalty between you and me. I also hope you like your gold crucifix necklaces, rosary, and the autobiography of St. Thérèse of Lisieux of France. Father said that he would translate the book to you.

I know a group of six Carmelite sisters. They call me family. I am going down to see them soon. I think a woman can aspire to nothing greater than being a nun in a Carmelite monastery. We are great friends and laugh a lot. The story of St. Thérèse of Lisieux is a story of a Carmelite nun like these sisters.

My husband, Jack, is a saint in my opinion, but not in his. I love him very much. We have a beautiful older dog named Lady.

You sign your letters "daughter," and I love it; but should I refer to myself as your mom, because you have had one mother? I would love to be called your mom if it would not hurt your feelings.

I love you, dearest Margaret.
Mary Faith

December 21, 1996

Dearest and beloved daughter Margaret,

Margaret, I was very happy to receive your letter [letter is lost]. I am so proud of you for studying so hard. I assume you are in primary six by now. However, if you are not, you did your best and that is what matters to me. I do believe you can do anything you set your mind and heart to.

I am glad you liked your birthday presents enough to consider them a dream. Every young woman should have a dream come true. I know by now you have the mattress, etc. I hope you already have the bed I sent money for.

Dearest Margaret, what do you mean when you say you want to be a girl of God? Do you want to become a nun and a bride of Christ? I would be more than overjoyed if this were true. However, it is between you and God.

Is someone translating St. Thérèse's *Story of a Soul* to you? I hope so. By the way, I sent a copy to your brother.

The Carmelite sisters gave me for Christmas the most beautiful Christmas tree ornaments. They were all handmade by them, and that makes them very precious to me. Included were cinnamon sticks tied up in lace and ornaments made with dried roses. The room smells wonderful. What a happy and loving surprise.

There is a very strong need for good nuns in this country. The sisters in Springfield keep praying for a suitable new young nun. I would hope you would pray to God about this. I think you would be perfect for them, and they would be perfect for you. And even with vows of poverty, chastity, and obedience, their external life is so much easier here. They do practice prayer, penance, and sacrifice for the salvation of souls and sinners. But this vocation is between you and God. Even though you are only thirteen, I think you are very mature for your age and know your own mind. I should not push you. Margaret, I want you to know that whatever you do with your life, your mum will always love you deeply.

Yours in the love of Christ,
Your mum, Mary Faith

1997

November 24, 1997

Dearest Margaret,

Congratulations! Every time you write to me, your English is better. I know you are working very hard.

I am very sorry I have not written to you in a long while. I have been sick, but I am fine now. I am very sorry you are suffering in your world. Keep your dream alive. I pray for your vocation all the time.

I am keeping this letter short, because I am sending you a copy of an article that was in a Springfield, Missouri, magazine on the Carmelite sisters.

I love you very much.

Mary Faith

1998

February 9, 1998

Dearest Margaret,

I am your mum, and you are my child, and I love you. I love you. I love you. I will always and forever love you.

You have told me [letter lost] that it is your dream to join the Carmelite Sisters. Every day I offer up prayers, works, joys, and sufferings for your vocation.

How are you doing in school? I know you are an excellent student.

Yours in Christ,
Mary Faith, your mum

June 28, 1998

Dear Mary Faith,

Warm greetings to you from your beloved daughter Margaret. I am now in my second term of primary seven (p.7) and I will complete primary school in November. And do not forget to pray for me so that I can perform very well. I have been sick suffering from malaria. I will write to you more often. Let me end hereby wishing you the best in whatever you are doing.

Your beloved daughter,
Margaret

July 1998

Dear Mary Faith

My best friend Mary. I am so happy to write to you. How are you my friend? For me, I have been in the holidays but attending daily the church because I want to be confirmed as a Christian in the church. But my dear friend, I am sorry to inform you that my mother is seriously sick and bed-ridden. She can pass-away anytime. So try to pray for me to be firm. Thanks for helping with everything, even for sponsoring me. I am so happy. Nowadays we are busy as it is the rainy season so I have prepared a garden for beans and cassava.

Your loving daughter,
Margaret

P.S. My mother died on the following day and we buried her, so pray for me.

August 1998

Dear Mary Faith

I wish to write and know how you are.

Convey my warm greetings to your husband, Jack. Tell him I love him very much. I personally I am doing well. The studies are hard. But I promise you that I will try my best. Now we are studying at primary school with my brother Vincent. The Fathers took us to the school after the death of our second parent because we had no one to look after us. I am now in P.5. I repeated it because all my time was spent on my mother looking after her. Now I assure that I will perform well and be promoted to P.6. I once again thank you for all you do for me. Thank you very much, and may God bless you and your work.

I remain your beloved daughter,
Margaret

September 10, 1998

Dearest Margaret,

Dear heart, I received your picture. You looked like an American girl with your new dress, backpack, and bright shiny shoes.

Your priest wrote me and said that you are aspiring to join a congregation of Carmelite sisters. What a grace it would be to have a vocation to Carmel. I think you would enjoy the community of the sisters. However, I hope you realize that the focus of the Carmelites is prayer, sacrifice, and penance to redeem sinners that might otherwise go to hell by becoming a channel of grace for them. If you have a vocation to Carmel, you will be very happy in this life, and God will greatly reward you through all eternity.

Dearest Margaret, if you have any questions in your mind about your vocation in the far future, you should consider it in depth. However, at the age of fifteen, relax and let God work in your soul. Give yourself a break. Carmel, I believe, will accept you. You will need to wait until you are eighteen to enter. Carmelite life is a marvelous life. You should consider your education now. In that way, if you enter Carmel and do not have a vocation, you will have an education to fall back on. I will continue to support you in your education. However, I would be very pleased if you truly have a vocation to Carmel.

It is a rare gift from God. Then too, there are easier sisterhoods.

I know you want to become an American citizen and join the Carmelites over here. Now, there are three ways to become an American. You can marry an American, be selected for a visa from the visa lottery, or you may join one of the American military services for three years.

Women are not sent to positions to fight, even during periods of war. You would be safe. While in the military, you would receive good food, good lodging (heating and air-conditioning), and every medical and dental need would be taken care of. You would be given free education while you are in the military.

To join the military, you only need to pass a simple English and math test. Already, your English is better than that of some Americans. How are you doing in math? After your three years in the military, you would be able to be an American citizen. You also would be given thousands and thousands of dollars for future education, if you want it. Or you would be able to join the Carmelites in the United States. You could do anything you want.

May God bless you in the peace of Christ,
Mary Faith, your mum

November 1998

Dearest Mary Faith,

Thank you very much for the nice article on the Carmelite sisters. I have been reading it slowly and meditating upon its contents. I am sure it will help me develop more my thoughts of taking on this vocation.

I am now in my first term in primary seven this year I will be sitting for national exams (primary leaving exams) and completing the primary school level. Pray for me as I work hard.

God bless you and keep you.
Your beloved daughter,
Margaret

December 1998

Dear Mum Mary Faith,

I wish to inform you that I am doing well with my studies and I want to become a girl of God. Mum, thank you very much for my gifts and my funds. I was very happy when I received them. It was a dream to me. Father bought me a ream of paper. You are really so good to me and I love you, too. In addition, we are about to do our final exams. Mum, I wish to promise you that I will try my best to pass them. Mum, Father told me that you sent me money to buy my personal needs. Mum, I do not know how I can thank you; it's only God who will pay you. Mum, as we are about to come to Christmas time, let me wish you the best on that day and happy new year's. Thank you very much for your letter and photo. I liked it, Mum. Mum, I love you.

I remain your beloved daughter,
Margaret

1999

February 22, 1999

My dear Margaret,

My love, one of the reasons I want you to join the Carmelite monastery in Springfield, Missouri, is because you would be close. You would only be 150 miles away, and they would allow me to see you once a year. I miss you as any mother would miss her daughter.

Any time Father or you want to telephone me, you can do so by calling me "collect." When a person calls collect, it means the other person pays for the charges. If you need anything or want to talk to me, have Father tell the international operator that you want to call collect. Call when you wish, but remember during daylight hours here I might not be home occasionally. Just keep trying to reach me. Call me when you get this letter. I hope you are well and your studies are coming along. I await your call.

In the love of Christ,
Your mum, Mary Faith

March 1999

Dear Mary Faith,

I am very happy to write to you. How are you and Jack? Thank you very much for my gifts.

My brother, Vincent, is studying hard, as well. We are only two children in the family. Once again thank you very much for what you do for me.

May God bless you,

I remain your beloved daughter,
Margaret

July 25, 1999

My dearest Margaret,

Thank you for asking how we are. My husband is very much overworked, but he likes his job very much. I am fine. Our two-year-old dog, Lady Regina, is spoiled to death.

I am thrilled that Vincent has entered the seminary. Just think, two vocations in one family!

I am glad that your classes are going well. As always, I love you and wish you were here.

In the love of Christ Jesus,
Your mum, Mary Faith

September 20, 1999

Dearest Mum Mary Faith,

It is really a great joy and pleasure to being sponsored. This time at least to say a word of hello to you. How are you and Jack? I am sorry to hear your two-year-old dog Lady Regina was spoiled to death.

I am okay. In the first place, I wish to thank you for all the good-hearted things you render to me always. Thank you for the $220 donated to me for buying textbooks, reams of papers, sheets, dresses, shoes, etc. I received them and they have sincerely helped me very much. The textbooks have contributed much to the success of my studies as I discover new things from them. Let me also use this chance to inform you that the smooth running of the school has contributed much to my academic performance, loving and knowing my God, and even the entire generation.

I wish to stop here by asking the almighty God to bless you and Jack.

> I remain your beloved daughter,
> Margaret

November 27, 1999

My dearest Margaret,

How have you been? I hope school is still going well and not too hard. Do you have a lot of homework to do?

Do you hear from Vincent? How is he doing at the seminary?

Father told me the weather where you are is about eighty-six degrees year round. We have changing seasons here. It is now well into the fall time of the year. In fall, the leaves of the trees turn bright colors and then drop to the ground. The trees are practically bare now. We had our first frost a month ago. We will now have about three months of winter.

It snows once or twice a year. Temperatures sometimes get down to zero degrees. In March, we sometimes see the first signs of spring. My favorite time of the year is spring. The trees look like they have green lace on them. This lace develops into full-blown leaves and the flowers begin to bloom. It is usually rainy in April or May, then the summer heat hits. It usually gets up to about ninety-two degrees. Then in September, fall begins again.

What are you doing for fun and relaxation? I hope you do not have to go to school all the time. As always, I love you. In the love of Christ Jesus,

> Your mum, Mary Faith

December 1999

Dear Mary Faith,

With great pleasure, may I take this opportunity to send you and Jack my greetings through the mighty name of our Lord Jesus Christ. How are you? May I take this very chance to send my sincere thanks to you all who helped me in all my daily struggle up to this point. It is my prayer that you also stay in good health and have a happy life together.

Thanks for all the endeavors you send to me also. I wish you a Merry Christmas and Happy New Year.

Yours faithfully,
Your Daughter Margaret

2000

January 2000

Dear Mary Faith,

How are you and Jack? On my side I am all fantastic and the studies are going on smoothly. Mum, how is the atmosphere over there?

Let me take this time to thank you for the great effort you take towards my education. In fact, I have nothing to reward you with. I put you in my daily prayers. May the Lord bless and keep you.

Your beloved daughter,
Margaret

February 2000

Dear Mum,

I hope you are fine. Last year I was very happy to receive your letter. I am busy with my studies. Mum I thank you for the work you have done for me. And me, I must study very hard. And I thank you for the good things you send to me. I am so happy to receive those. Last year I wrote you a letter that I must become a sister. I am sure of that. Pray for me, so that I can study hard. And let me pray for you so that you can get money for my fees. So that I can keep my promises, I just pray to God day to day, trying to beg Him for my needs. One day, He will answer my prayers. Mum, I am trying my level best to reach where I want to go with my studies. I will be in that good life where you are without suffering in this world. So pray for me. I will never forget you in my prayers. That is a fact. I wish you great greetings to you.

Yours sincerely,
Margaret

March 26, 2000

My dearest Margaret,

Congratulations, Margaret, on being promoted again. How is Vincent doing in his studies? How often do you see him?

I am enclosing two holy cards. I will let you decide which one you want to keep for yourself and which one you want to give to Vincent. Also enclosed is a wallet-size picture of my husband, Jack, myself, and our dog, Lady Regina, a picture of Monsignor (who I have known since 1971), and a close up of Lady Regina's head. Monsignor and I are good friends and talk on the telephone long distance. We can talk either seriously about religion or tell jokes to or about each other. A monsignor is between a priest and a bishop.

In the United States, our English includes slang phrases. When I said that we spoiled Lady Regina to death, I meant that we treat her very well. She is very much alive. She just celebrated her third birthday.

In the love of Christ Jesus,
Your mum,
Mary Faith

April 2000

Dearest Mum Mary Faith,

With a great pleasure may I take this opportunity to send you my greetings through the mighty name of our Lord Jesus Christ.

Thank you very much for your sponsorship. Thanks for the Christmas party contribution you sent last year.

I do want to join the Carmelite monastery you talked about in the letter.

I am with pleasure to inform you that I passed my primary leaving examination. I hope to perform better as time goes.

Let me end hereby wishing you the most joyful time this coming Easter.

Your loving daughter
Margaret

May 28, 2000

Dearest Margaret,

Pope John Paul II has called the United States of America

a culture of death. When a woman expecting a baby does not want the baby, she can legally have an operation to kill the baby. This is called an abortion. In some states, she is allowed to have a partial-birth abortion. In a partial-birth abortion, the woman can wait until she is giving birth. When the newborn baby's head comes out of the woman, the doctor takes an instrument, pushes it through the baby's brain, and kills the baby. About 4,000 abortions are done a day in this country. Pray for this country.

Margret, selfishly I wanted you near me in this country. Recently I found out the ages of the Carmelite nuns in Springfield, Missouri. These are the nuns that I am friends with. They range in age from thirty-nine to seventy-eight. I do not believe it would be healthy for you to join them. You are too young to be with nuns in this age range. There are only five nuns there. They have not had a sister take final vows in many, many years. I am afraid one of these days they will go back to St. Louis Monastery, where they originated.

In this country, there is a shortage of priests and nuns, partially due to the culture of death, which expands beyond abortions. Sex and violence are throughout television and the movies. God's name is taken in vain quite frequently.

I have talked to two priests that I know very well, and whose judgment I trust, about you coming over here to be a sister. Both are adamant that you would lose your vocation over here. I know this comes as a shock. Blame me. I came up with the idea of bringing you over here.

I hope you will continue your studies to the best of your abilities and join the Carmelite order near you. You have so much to give. I will continue to sponsor you, write to you, and try to be an unselfish mum. I do love you, Margaret. I pray for you and Vincent all the time. Pray to the one who is Mother to us both, the Blessed Virgin Mary.

Yours in Christ,

Mary Faith, your mum

September 13, 2000

Dear Mum, Mary Faith,

With a great pleasure let me take this opportunity to write to you through the name of our Lord Jesus Christ the almighty God. With that how are you? Back to me I am fine and everything is going on well.

Mum, I am so proud of you. I am thankful and grateful for your gift of the holy cards, your photo with Dad Jack, the photos of Lady Regina and Monsignor, and other prayer cards you enclosed. Thank you again for the money you sent to me for my dental care plus other school supplies. I am with an assurance that this will contribute much to keep my teeth well and even my studies to progress smoothly. You have given me the most relevant school supplies.

Vincent was also very much excited to receive the Holy Card sent to him. He is now fine and enjoys his vocation school well as he is so much devoted to become a priest. He has sent his warm greetings to you. I used to be with him during the holidays.

Mum, I am so sorry to hear about the prevailing culture of death in your country. Though it is again happening here in Uganda, but on a small rate. I am worried that through this practice we may lose so many people who may have become useful and important ones in future. Let us pray to the almighty God so that this practice is abolished completely. I am again happy to inform you that my studies are progressing well and I am looking forward to joining my third term in senior two.

I pray that my ambition of becoming a nun continues. I pray and think of you daily.

I remain your daughter,

Margaret

2001

January 2001

Dearest Mary Faith,

I greet you in the name of our Lord Jesus Christ. How was Christmas at large? It was fantastic for me.

I am so grateful for the three textbooks you sent. One was about *Heavenly Army of Angels* and the other one was about *Powerful Women in the Church* and the *Many Faces of Mary*, a love story, plus the funeral services card for Jack's mother. I was impressed to get to know more about her. May her soul rest in peace. I am happy to inform you that studies are going on well and I was promoted to S-2 this year. Thanks for your prayers and help. And also Vincent is fine and he is doing well. Before I pen off I want to thank you for the contribution you made towards the Christmas Party. Surely I had fun. We had a lot to eat and to drink. In fact it was successful.

Congratulations through the Millennium. May the Lord keep you and bless you.

From your beloved daughter,
Margaret

February 17, 2001

Dearest Margaret,

I received your letter some time ago, and I am sorry that it has taken so long to answer you. I pray for you and Vincent in particular every day, and for all those where you are, in general. I pray for your vocation to Carmel and for Vincent's vocation to the priesthood. Congratulations on being promoted again. Jack and I are very proud of you. You consistently do very well.

Yours in Christ,
Mary Faith, your mum

March 2001

Dearest Mum Mary Faith,

With great pleasure I greet you in the name of our Lord Jesus Christ. With that how is your life over there? First of all, I would like to thank you for the fantastic assistance you render to me often. I am so proud of you.

Mum I am with hope that you enjoyed the Christmas days plus the new holy year well. On my side it was successful and I enjoyed them in many ways.

Mum thank you for everything you have done to me which I cannot tell. It is a pleasure to inform you that this year I am in senior two and I am working hard so that I can be promoted to senior three. And I wish to continue working tirelessly so that everything goes on well. Let me pen off by wishing you a happy Easter and may the Lord keep you in peace.

From your beloved daughter,
Margaret

March 19, 2001

Dearest Margaret,

I understand you still desire to become a nun, and this makes Jack and me very happy.

We are also happy that Vincent is in the seminary.

We are beginning to see signs of spring. I saw a robin the other day. Traditionally, this bird heralds in the spring season.

I know you are doing well in your classes. You always work hard in your studies and are always promoted to the next level. Jack and I are both very proud of you.

We enjoy your artwork. Please write and let us know how you are doing and if you need anything.

In the love of Christ,
Mary Faith, your mum

May 2001

Dearest Mary Faith,

Let me pray to God that you are fine and I hope everything is going on well.

Mum, the reason of writing this letter is just to thank you for the help you offered for my dental care. I really am proud of that. And also I would like to thank you for the letters you sent. It made me so happy to hear from you and to get to know how you are doing.

Let me stop here for the time being and I always pray for you, for whatever you do for me. In fact I am very happy. Vincent sends greetings to you and to Jack.

From your beloved daughter,
Margaret

June 21, 2001

Dearest Margaret,

Can you believe that Pentecost has already gone by? Jack is doing well and working very hard. I had to have a total knee replacement. Yesterday we saw the doctor. He said that I was doing exceptionally well.

Did you have a vacation? I hope you did and had a good time. If you had a vacation, please write and tell us what you did.

I hope you are well. Study hard, pray hard, and play hard. Margaret, I love you, and God bless you.

In the love of Christ,
Mary Faith, your mum

June 2001

Dearest Mary Faith,

With a great pleasure let me hope that you are fine and I think everything you are doing is going on well. Back to me I personally, I am fine.

Mum the reason I am writing this letter is quite optimistic just to say a word of thanks through this gracious piece of paper. Mum in fact I do not know how I can show you my happiness but later on, I will show it to you through God's power.

Mum I think you know this year I am in senior three and I hope next year I will be finishing my O-level exam. So Mum your prayers are requested.

Mum let me pen off by wishing you the joy and happiness of all the world.

From your beloved daughter,
Margaret

November 25, 2001

Beloved Margaret,

I read that some people where you live are suffering from the disease of bubonic plague. Has anyone you know had this? I hope not.

Be assured that I am praying for you, Vincent, and your religious vocations. I pray that both of you find joy in the religious life.

Margaret, tell me about your friends in school and what you are studying.

We are sending two hundred American dollars to you as a Christmas present and for all your needs. I hope there will be a little money left over for you to spend on whatever you want. Both Jack and I wish you and Vincent a Merry Christmas and a Happy New Year.

In the love of Christ,
Mary Faith, your mum

December 2001

Dearest Mum Mary Faith,

This time I am very happy to send a few words of hello to you. In other words, how are you and Jack? Hope you are fine. Back to me. I am fine and everything is going on well.

Mum, thank you for the endeavors you shown me. In fact, Christmas was enjoyable and everything on that day went on successfully for in this case, people ate and drank and they forgot all their burdens. Bad enough we had no camera to send you a photo but I promise next time we shall send one.

I am proud of everything you do for me and I am still proud of the money you sent for clothes and other needs plus the Christmas preparations.

I am sure, Mum, I will do everything you need me to be or to become. I will not let you down.

I always pray for you. Let me stop here, with that I wish you a nice stay and send greetings to Jack that I love him very much.

Your beloved daughter,
Margaret

2002

February 10, 2002

Dearest Margaret,

I loved your Christmas card. The rose was so beautiful and realistic. I particularly liked the perfect shading you did on the rose in black. You are an excellent artist.

I hope you can continue your artwork after you enter the Carmelite monastery. The Carmelite sisters, I know, make beautiful cards giving people their prayers, works, and sacrifices for a donation. Perhaps you could do this in Carmel. If you are not allowed to draw in Carmel, do not be upset. Give to God this sacrifice, and He will look at the beautiful artistry of your soul.

Please start your Carmelite prayer life now and continue to pray for us. I pray for you and Vincent every day, many times a day. I pray for many, but you and Vincent are very close to my heart. I love you, Margaret, my beautiful, courageous, and darling daughter.

In the love of Christ,

Mary Faith, your mum

February 2002

Dearest beloved Mum Mary Faith,

I greet you in the name of our Lord Jesus Christ. Let me hope that everything is going on smoothly. How is Jack? I always think of him, and I will continue to pray for him. On my side I am okay and everything is going on well plus the studies. Mum with pleasure to inform you that this year I am going to finish my O level and I want to assure you that I have to get a 1st (first) grade in the name of Jesus Christ. It is a rainy season whereby the area is cold and people are busy planting crops and others cultivating land since we depend on farming and why people become happy during the rainy season.

I am wishing you a happy Easter mingled with joy of all heavens. For us we hope to enjoy our Easter at school.

Mum have a nice stay at home and a prosperous life. I love you mum.

From your beloved daughter,
Margaret

March 31, 2002

Dearest Margaret,

I am sending this letter to you at your school because I feel we can communicate faster this way. You can call us and it will not cost you or the school anything. This is called "calling collect." When you call us, tell the operator that you want to call collect to Jack or Mary.

By the way, Margaret, we were talking about the Carmelite monastery in our last letter. I just wanted to let you know that being in the Carmelite order is an excellent gift to God. However, that does not mean it is the most perfect thing for you. I want you to be happy in whatever you choose to do in life, whether it is being a Carmelite nun, the life of a nun in an easier order, or getting married. That is what you must do.

I hope everything is fine with you. Call us as soon as possible. In the meantime, we will write to you at the old address. We hope you are having a meaningful season.

In the love of Christ,
Mary Faith, your mum

March 18, 2002

Dearest beloved Mum Mary Faith

Mum, you may be surprised to see a different address from the usual one. I have written this letter from school and the reason as to why I have written this letter individually. I want to inform you that I would like you to send me your telephone number and Fax number. Please Mum reply through the above address so that I can tell you more. Lovely Mum, please do not stop writing to those in charge. Please write to them whenever you receive a letter.

May the good Lord bless you, Mum, and I love you.

From your beloved daughter,
Margaret

April 2002

Beloved Mum Mary Faith,

With a great pleasure, I would like to take this opportunity and say hello to you. With that, how is life and Jack?

First of all, I would like to thank you for your endeavors you always show me, most especially during my studying. With that I thank you again for the money you sent. In fact, it contributed to buy some textbooks, dresses, shoes, and other personal needs. I think God will keep you safe and healthy because in everything we do, we first pray to God.

About my friends at school, everybody is supposed to have a friend (best friend). But the most formidable thing is that you get a friend and she can become your enemy. But not all friends are like that. Most of them pray to God, so that they can get a heart of loving others. Well Mum I am planning to become "a nun" (sister). I think I will become one due to the reason being that religious leaders most of them have a heart of helping others.

They have nothing much disturbing them like producing children.

Mum I love you. May God bless you.

From your beloved daughter,
Margaret

May 2002

Dearest Mum Mary Faith,

Hope you are okay and I think everything you do is going on smoothly. I am fine and everything is going on well, especially in the field of studies. I am just back from my holidays. It is now raining and people are busy planting crops.

Besides that, I am working hard since this term is the promotional term and next year I think I will become a candidate. Please Mum I need your prayers as I always do. Allow me to stop here. May the Lord bless you with good life. But please convey my greetings to all your pals and relatives, most especially, Jack.

From your beloved daughter,
Margaret

June 3, 2002

Dearest Margaret,

You wrote and indicated that something troublesome may have happened to you. Bring all the bad in your life to me and Mother Mary, who is the mother of us all. She will comfort you as I try to. Often, I pray for you and Vincent every day, many times a day.

When the worst things happen, I go to Jesus and literally hold out my hand in bed at night for Him to hold spiritually. He comforts me. I hope you will go to Mary, the Father, the Son, and the Holy Spirit to be comforted. Come to me.

In whatever you do, don't blame God or the Blessed Virgin Mary for anything that happens to you. God is all good and all loving. He will never hurt you. The devil will try to make you turn against God because life is hard. It is not God's fault. It is the fault of the devil and Adam. They wanted to be gods. Ever since then, we live in a world capable of much evil. But God, the Blessed Virgin Mary, and I love you no matter what happens. I love you always. Always come to me with your troubles. God loves you so very much, Margaret, more than any of us will ever know.

I read in your last letter about the girl who was your best friend but became your enemy. God told us to love and pray for our enemies. I have been trying to do this for my part; I am in much the same situation. Jack says a neighbor up the street is jealous of me. With one hand she pats my shoulder and with the other she knifes me in the back. Perhaps the young lady you are talking about sees the things you get from us and she is jealous. She is your cross. Christ told us we would have a cross to carry as well. For now try not to let her upset you. The devil would be delighted to see you upset. He knows how good you are. He knows how much good you can do in the Carmelite monastery for others in the world. The devil will work hard to keep you from being a Carmelite nun, but remember, there will be many people in the world praying for your vocation. There will be great joy in your vocation as well as hardship. Jack and I will always, always love you.

In the love of Christ,
Mary Faith, your mum

August 30, 2002

Dear Father,

We received a telephone call today from the foundation telling us not to send extra money, other than our monthly amount, to Margaret, our sponsored child. They said that it makes other children jealous.

We understand that she is now attending a boarding school. We are concerned that if we can no longer send her extra money that she may have to leave the school. We have corresponded with Margaret for several years regarding her desire to enter a Carmelite monastery. My wife talked to one of the staff members at the foundation about the possibility of Margaret becoming a Carmelite nun now. We would then contribute to the whole monastery. My wife is friends with some Carmelites and knows a person can enter at Margaret's age.

Could you call us and talk to us about this situation, please.

In the love of Christ,
Jack and Mary Faith

September 10, 2002

My Dearest Margaret,

I have the unfortunate duty to send my almost-grown daughter some bad news. The foundation informed us that we can no longer send you more money than the twenty-dollars-a-month sponsorship fee. We cannot send $100 for your birthday and we cannot send $200 for Christmas. The reason they gave was that some of the girls might see Father giving you presents that they do not get and become jealous. I told them to let the other sponsors know how little the twenty dollars goes with the hope they would send in more for their sponsored children. They, in turn, said to me that there would be some children whose sponsors could not afford more than the twenty dollars a month.

When I was about twenty-five years old, I frequently went to Monsignor who was my spiritual director. Monsignor and I talk on the telephone to this day. However, at the time, he did not feel it was proper for a priest and a young lady to be getting together so often because there was a rumor going around the parish that I was having his baby. I have never had anyone's baby, including Jack's. Jack and I could not have children. So I was not able to see much of Monsignor until many years later. Now, both Jack and I go to see Monsignor where he lives in another town. Look what happened because of vicious rumors.

Now back to you, Margaret. You can see what jealousy can do. There is another reason that I believe they don't want Father giving you things he can't give to the other girls. There is a crisis in the church right now involving priests who are now, or who have in the past, treated children and young teenagers in the wrong way. The Pope has said that all priests who do such things can no longer be priests. Thus, you can see Margaret that the Fathers do not want to appear that there is something special going on between you and either of them. If one of the jealous girls came up with an idea like this and spread it around, both of them could lose their priesthood.

Thank you so much for the unbelievably beautiful table

runner and place mats. I cannot believe how beautiful it is and how well it was done. It is perfect. You certainly have talent in your drawing and your crocheting. These are the gifts God has given to you. I talked to the foundation and they said that if you enter the Carmelite monastery, that Jack and I can give as much as we want to the monastery.

In the sixteenth century, Saint Teresa of Avila in Spain reformed the Carmelite monastery to be what it is today. Previously it had been no more than a social club. Now the nuns wear habits and sandals, don't talk unless necessary, but have a great time in recreation when they do talk and laugh. They are totally self-sufficient. That means they grow their own vegetables and accept donations of money.

Saint Teresa also limited the size of each monastery to no more than twenty-one sisters. The Carmelite sisters I know have five sisters in their monastery. The three hundred dollars a year we give will go a long way for twenty-one or fewer sisters, and they also have other people to rely on for donations.

Once again, we would give to the monastery $300, and as one of the sisters, you would benefit. After talking to the sisters I know in the United States, I believe that you qualify to enter the monastery now. So it is up to you, Margaret, when you enter the Carmelite monastery in Africa. You will be taken care of. Jack and I will take care of you as we always have. In the love of Christ,

Mary Faith, your mum

October 2, 2002

Beloved Mum Mary Faith,

With a great pleasure let me take this opportunity to say a word of hello to you. Hope life is okay and let me pray to God that everything you are doing is going on well. Mum I have written this letter to express my sincere gratitude for your caring kindness, loving, and sacrifice for me. With that I am sorry for taking long to write to you due to some inconveniences I had. Some of them are as follows.

First, I tried to call you using my pocket money when going to school. Mum, I stay with nothing, because the operator charged me a lot of money and I ended up staying in school with nothing. At school, they don't visit me and yet they give me very little money. Mum I am suggesting that if possible you can send me some money through the letters. I think I will be able to receive it because, Mum, I need much to buy for myself and I am given little.

Mum I also want to plan, you and me so that in my vacation I can come to your place. In fact Mum I am tired of living in Uganda. I want to stay with you Mum. Do not let me down because you are the only person I want to stay with in this world. Besides, we are soon seating for our O-level leaving examinations, but please, Mum, remember to pray for me. Mum, I am eagerly waiting for your letter. Every person at school is waiting to see what is coming from my Mum. Mum I fear to tell much because you may be disgusted. Please try to write to me as soon as possible, because after finishing our examinations, we will be leaving the school. Tell me what you are suggesting.

I have much to tell you. Mum I am bankrupt. Please try to send me some money at school. I am sorry, Mum. Thank you for the letters you wrote to me. I am wishing you and Jack good times.

> God bless you, from your beloved daughter,
> Margaret

October 11, 2002

Dearest Margaret,

Jack and I got your letter. We can understand why you want to leave Uganda, but this cannot happen overnight.

We will support you as we said. Jack and I have talked it over, and we have agreed to send you thirty-five dollars a month total. Margaret, my medical problems have taken most of our money. As you know, we send money monthly to the foundation for you. We would like to send an additional fifteen dollars directly to you which we will try to convert into Ugandan currency. We need to know what kind of currency is used in Uganda. Please write and tell us. At this time, the foundation will not let us send more than the regular sponsorship fee monthly for you through them. This is the most we can afford to send you at this time. We hope that we can send more to you someday. I have had seven surgeries in the last year and a half and need one more. I didn't tell you about all my problems because I didn't want you to worry about me. The surgeries that I have had are not life-threatening but are very, very painful, so please keep me in your prayers. I am taking very strong pain medicines.

Do you have another year in school? I looked into your coming to the United States. A person can come from Uganda to the United States under two conditions. The first is that the person is being persecuted in their country. That is not your situation. The second situation is to come to the United States for a short period of time to study, promising your home country (Uganda) that you will return home after finishing your studies. Father came to the US for three years to study before going back to Uganda. In order to fly to the United States, it will cost $3,220 for a one-way ticket, and someone your age should not fly alone. So it would cost $6,440. Perhaps you could come to the United States when Father is coming to seek donations. It is a long trip. In order to get here, you will have to spend a total of twenty-five hours in the air. You will have to stay overnight in Amsterdam. You will have to travel 10,070 miles in the air.

I talked to a man at the Catholic college here in my city and he said they have a program for foreign students. It will cost $12,000 for the first two terms. We cannot afford this. However, when I talked to the man at the college, he thought there might be some kind of help available for you. I just pray that the school might have a scholarship program for overseas students. We will write soon and try to forward fifteen dollars to you. We are not supposed to send money in the mail because it will be stolen. We will try to do it this time.

In the love of Christ,
Mary Faith, your mum

October 15, 2002

Beloved Margaret,

I could not find a bank with shillings. Go to Father, if possible, to exchange money into shillings. Don't let the jealous girls or anyone else know you have American money for your safety's sake.

God bless you.
Mary Faith

P.S. I hope this helps. Please let me know as soon as possible so we can send more.

October 30, 2002

Dearest Mum Mary Faith,

Let me pray to God that you are fine. On my side everything is okay most especially my studies are going on smoothly as you may know that in October I am beginning my O-level examinations and please keep me in your prayers as they are greatly welcome. First of all, I would like to thank you for the letter you sent to me. I was very happy because I could not expect that.

We are now in the rainy season, people are busy growing crops and I think in my vacation I will do the same. You know Ugandans depend on farming.

Mum hope you are well. I will continue to pray to God for you.

Let me stop here, and here are greetings from Vincent. He loves you so much.

God bless you abundantly.

From your beloved daughter,
Margaret

November 1, 2002

Dearest Mum Mary Faith,

Let me take this opportunity to say a word of hi to you. Hope life is okay and everything you do is fantastic. Back to me, I am filled with joy of all heavens due to the money you sent to me. In fact, I am still proud.

For the $100 you sent (graduation gift), I bought some nice dresses, shoes plus some other needs. Mum it's only God who knows and what to do for you. I am a person who is enjoying the fruits of the earth, because I receive everything that I need. I know Mum it's you who has endowed to hold my studies up to this stage. Nothing I request from you do you delay to send it. Anyway, I don't know how I can say a word of thanks to you but

I will just hand you over to God because he is the final judge. Let me continue to pray to God that you get everything you ask from him and I think he will listen to you.

I don't have much to say but I am only wishing you a nice stay at home. God bless you plus Jack.

From your beloved daughter,
Margaret

November 9, 2002

Dearest beloved Margaret,

I am sending you more money. Per last month's letter, don't tell the jealous girls or anybody else except the Fathers about the money. If you do you could be risking your own life. Do whatever you were able to do to cash the last installment of money into shillings. Tell me what you had to do last time to change the money.

You will receive the same amount of money at the same time in December. From what you wrote about what you bought with October's installment of money it sounds like you are in pretty good shape financially. Always use the money to buy what you need. However, if there is any left over, give a little to God. The Bible says to do this. Save as much money as you can for college, for a house, or to give the Carmelites when you enter the monastery. You will receive more money next month and every month. Please pray for Jack and me.

I love you. I love you. I love you, and I am so proud of you. I could not have a better daughter than you.

Much love in Christ.
Your beloved mum, Mary Faith

December 13, 2002

Dear Fathers,

I tried to call you for hours according to my husband's instructions. He was trying to help because I thought I had written the time down wrong. Among the three of us, Vincent, Margaret, and I are disappointed.

Could we try again? I will be much more careful about getting the correct call time. Soon enough Vincent will have a parish of his own, and I will not be able to speak to Margaret in the Carmelite monastery.

Please forgive me, Fathers, for putting you through a lot of work for nothing.

Yours in our Lord,
Mary Faith

December 24, 2002

Dearest Margaret,

Throughout the years, I have wanted you to have the things a young lady in the United States would have. In a way, I am responsible for making your schoolmates jealous of you. They are doing what comes naturally; they want what you have. They are jealous. We can understand this. However, it does not mean they are doing the right thing, the supernatural thing, and the grace-filled thing. I would hope you would look at them and see Jesus. He said, "Whatever you do to the least of my brethren, that you do unto me." He also asked us to pray for and do good to those that hurt us. I am sending thirty dollars for two months. In addition, I have included fifteen dollars for the girls who want what you have. In the spirit of Christ, go to them and split the last fifteen dollars among them.

Ask each young lady what she would like.

Merry Christmas and Happy New Year
Mary Faith

P.S. I should be very grateful due to a little Christmas cross. Crosses are a source of great blessings.

2003

February 22, 2003

Dearest Margaret,

I don't know how much you know about this, but I called one of the priests to see how you were doing, and he told me that you had left school for a week's vacation to visit relatives. I know Vincent is your only relative. Isn't he in the same city as you are? I thought he was. I also thought back to the time you said you hated living in Uganda. This was the same time that we sent you forty-five dollars in American money. All things considered, I thought you had run away to try to get out of Uganda to get to a nicer place.

For two or three days, I was very worried about you. Then a calm came upon me and I knew you would be all right because I knew that God was watching over you and protecting you. I called Father to see if there was any word about you, and he told me it was all a mistake, that he had confused you with another young lady. I was very happy to hear that you were all right and that you were doing what you were supposed to do, being a student in your school.

What did you decide to do with the extra fifteen dollars I sent you for the jealous girls? Margaret, my suggestion that you split the money among them was only a suggestion. I want you to feel free to do what you think is right in your conscience. You can always come to me and tell me your problems and I will offer you suggestions. But you are a young lady now and you need freedom to make up your own mind as to what is right. Don't keep me in the dark about anything, because you can trust me with everything you believe and think. You know I love you.

Margaret, we are sending you thirty dollars for February and March. Father said that you were sending an acknowledgement of the forty-five dollars that we sent you. I always ask you to send me word that you received the money all right. I want you to write me every month that we send you money and let us know you got it. I never received the acknowledgement that Father said was coming. Enough time has passed that if you sent the letter directly to us, we should have received it by now.

As I said, we are sending you thirty dollars for February and March. To make sure you are receiving the money and that no one else is getting it, I want to hear from you shortly. If I don't hear from you by the middle of April, I will assume that you are not receiving the money and someone else is. Then we will start making our contributions through the foundation. If you want us to continue sending you American dollars in cash, please drop us a short note that you have received the money. I know you are busy with your schoolwork. Jack and I love you. please write to us.

God bless you, my daughter.

In the love of Christ,
Your mum, Mary Faith

June 2, 2003

Dearest Mum Mary Faith,

I greet you in the name of our Lord Jesus Christ. Hope you're fine. Back to me I am fine.

Mum, I would like to express my sincere thanks to you for the things you always give me. First of all, I am studying because of you and I don't think I would get someone to help me like you. Mum, may God bless you.

I am with pleasure to inform you that I passed my Uganda certificate of examinations last year. This has helped me to join an advanced level still at my former school. All my target is to continue working hard so that I become a very good citizen in this world.

I don't have much to say.

I am wishing you the joy of all heavens.

All in love, from your beloved daughter,
Margaret

June 14, 2003

Dearest Margaret,

Did you ever receive the forty-five dollars we sent you or the thirty-five we sent last time? Please answer my question. I write you and I ask you questions and you write me good letters about other things when I really need to know the answers to the questions I ask you. You are a very good young woman, and I am not mad at you. But it is a little frustrating. So please answer my questions.

I have nothing but praise for you on how well you are doing in your studies. I am so proud of you that you received your certificate. I had a talk with someone at the foundation and she told me that you need $500 a year for two more years of schooling. Would these two years be at the college level?

I hope you are still planning on becoming a Carmelite nun. You could do no better thing with yourself than to offer yourself to God as a bride of Christ in the Carmelite monastery. You could also become his bride in an easier religious order.

If you have given up on the idea of becoming a nun, we will try to send you to college. We are told you need two more years of school and that each year will cost $500. I am trying to think of ways to raise the money for you for college. I have asked a number of my friends and relatives to give up sending me birthday presents in exchange for money for you for college.

All my surgeries have taken quite a toll on the funds that Jack and I have. However, we will do our best to see you get a college education.

I would like to suggest while you are in college that you continue to study English and that you add French and Spanish as your main course of study. If you were to become fluent in these three languages, after college you could go to a city in Uganda and become an airline flight attendant. An airline flight attendant is a person who works for the airline and helps take care of the passengers on the airplane. In this way, you would probably get to see a great deal of the world and perhaps the United States.

And if you could not become an airline flight attendant and you could speak a number of languages very well, you could work at hotels catering to people from abroad. Both positions should pay very well. What do you think?

Please answer my questions and send me a letter as soon as possible. Don't wait until you are asked to write me at Christmas time. In the picture you sent to me, I can see that you have grown up to be a beautiful young lady in your blue suit and gold shoes.

You look quite pretty. You have a beautiful smile on your face, and you look happy. I hope you are.

In the love of Christ,
Mary Faith, your mum

August 2, 2003

Dearest Mum Mary Faith,

With great pleasure, let me take this opportunity to say dear word to you. Hope life is treating you well. I am in a good state and everything I am doing is going on well. First of all, Mum, I thank you for the endeavors you did. You sent me forty-five dollars and thirty-five dollars. I received them well and a lot of things were planned for and helped me in school. But all in all, I thank you very much, Mum. May the good Lord reward you in whatever you do, most especially on my side.

Mum, about becoming the Carmelite sister, I am still aiming at that and I want to answer you that nothing can provoke me from becoming a Carmelite sister. In that I wanted to first complete my advanced level which you called a college level, so that I can join the Carmelite in the fruitful age whereby at that stage someone can decide maturely and can work better than that one who did not complete the advanced level. So Mum, I am now in senior five at my former school. In this case I am remaining with only one year to finish my advanced level.

For your suggestions, you talked about becoming an airline flight attendant or working at hotels catering to people from abroad. It is very good and I appreciate your view, only that at school, they do not teach Spanish. They teach, however, other languages like French and English. They teach them and I will make sure that I learn them all before completing my advanced level.

Let me pen off. May the Lord protect you in everything you do. I love you, Mum.

Greetings to Jack. I love him very much.

From your beloved daughter,
Margaret

September 20, 2003

Beloved Mum Mary Faith,

How is life? Hope everything you do is going on well. I am in a good state and everything is going on well, most especially on the side of studies. I remain with only one year in school. After completing my advanced level, I will be joining the Carmelite sisters.

Mum, I have sent you a basket and a "kef." One is for Jack. That is a "kef." The basket is for you Mum to put on the table for decoration. I will make more for you and Jack. I love him very much and I pray so that we can see each other eye to eye.

Let me pen off. Here are some greetings from Vincent he loves you very much. I wish you a nice stay filled with joy.

From your beloved daughter,
Margaret

September 20, 2003

Beloved Mum,

I am sorry but could you please write to me at school.

You may wonder why I did not say thank you for the fifteen dollars you sent, but I received it well. Please, if possible, you can continue the same. Thank you, Mum.

I think people at the post office are faithful and they cannot steal the money.

Mum, I lost contact with you, and I want to get it back.

From your beloved daughter,
Margaret

October 27, 2003

Dearest Mum Mary Faith,

With great pleasure I take this opportunity to say a word of hi to you! Hope life is good. Back to me, I am bogged down with books, and I want to assure you that I will try my level best to pass my examinations at the advanced level.

Mum, I want to tell you that I am proud of you now and whenever I receive your letter. I can spend a sleepless night thinking about you. Most especially thanks to God who has endeavored to protect you during day and night.

At our school, we have got the AIDS Youth Challenge Club. It teaches about the infection and the prevention of AIDS. So I decided to join that club because many youths are dying every day. So we go around visiting the youths; teaching them about AIDS. At home, I managed to grow some cassava, beans and maize but most of the time I spent at school. I sacrificed some time to grow some crops because some people in our community cannot afford to grow such crops and they end up not eating anything through the whole day, so I try to distribute the little to them.

With that, I don't have much to say, but here are some greetings from Vincent. He also joined the advanced level. He is also capable of making it.

Mum, allow me to pen off. May the good Lord keep you in peace. Stay cool and safe. I love you, Mum. Greetings to Jack. I will never forget him in my life and I think as time goes on, you and I shall meet. I just pray to God because he is the controller of everything.

From your beloved daughter,
Margaret

November 22, 2003

Dearest Margaret,

I received your beautiful blue and white basket. I keep your basket on my bedside table so I can see it and think of you often. Jack thought the rabbit was made in an excellent way, and he has it displayed proudly on a shelf in his office.

When you say nothing will provoke you from going to the Carmelites, I don't understand what you mean. Do you want to go or not? Your English is excellent now, but the word "provoke" is used in a different way in the English language. I'm very proud of you for doing so well with your studies, and I'm also proud of you for joining the AIDS Youth Challenge.

Even though others have hurt you, you have a very loving heart and soul. I can't tell you how proud I am of you.

I'm sure you and Vincent are doing great with your studies; you're both very intelligent. You are a beautiful artist. Your artistic talent will be a great addition to the convent, if you decide to go. I love and pray for you and Vincent every day, sometimes many times a day. How is he doing?

I am sending you sixty-five dollars for Christmas. I am going to sell some things to a friend and will send you more later.

Maybe if you share part of it with the young girls who have been jealous of you, they will be better toward you. But you cannot buy friends.

Again, I love you, Margaret.

In the love of Christ,
Mary Faith, your mum

2004

March 2004

Dearest Mary Faith,

With great pleasure I take this opportunity to say a word of hi to you. Hope life is treating you well. As for the pen gripper, I am in a good state. The books are becoming hard as I come towards the end. Through God's prayers, I will make it.

Mum, I don't have much to say, but I wish you a happy Easter. Hope you will enjoy it; we shall also enjoy it at school. You know, mum, Easter at school we celebrate it in a special way. This is because the head teacher of our school is a nun.

Whenever I look at her, I reflect on my future career. The nuns at school love me so much, because I told them that I am going to become a Carmelite sister. They became very much excited.

Still I wish you a happy Easter in advance. May the good Lord, who protects many of his people, protect you.

Greetings to Jack, I love him so much, and so I cannot forget sending him greetings.

May the Lord be with you.

From your beloved daughter,
Margaret

March 28, 2004

Dear Margaret,

Thank you for your last letter. Again, your gift of the basket was so loving, and so professionally done. As usual, I am also so proud of you for always being promoted in your studies. I don't believe that you have ever been held back.

Do you realize that in May, I will have been sponsoring you for ten wonderful years? I couldn't think of anyone who I would want more or I would love more.

Are you still in the AIDS Challenge? It seems strange to me that young people in your city are dying of AIDS, since that is where AIDS began. Don't the teenagers know how their parents died? I am very proud that you are helping your fellow students and telling them about the AIDS Challenge.

I pray for you, Margaret, every morning. I love you and I always will and so will Jack.

In the name of our Lord, Jesus Christ,
Mary Faith, your mum

April 2004

Beloved Mum Mary Faith,

Mum, I am very proud of the photograph of you, holding the basket I made for you.

In the letter you wrote to me you asked me what I meant about something that cannot "provoke" me. I think I used a wrong vocabulary word. What I meant is that nothing can stop me from becoming a Carmelite sister. In fact, Mum, I don't know whether I will sleep on the day when I join the college. Because whenever I tell my friends at school that I am going to become a Carmelite sister, they become proud of me because most of them said that they cannot manage being in a college. Students say that becoming a Carmelite sister is a gift from God, so it seems I also share that gift.

On a good note, Mum, I am going to get a certificate in the AIDS Youth Challenge, and I will be qualified to go and teach others about AIDS. You know, it is the greatest killer disease in Uganda and kills young and old alike.

Mum, thank you for the sixty-five dollars you sent to me for Christmas. In fact, I enjoyed the Christmas celebrations because they brought me new things like dresses, shoes, and many others.

In addition to that, in my school I am the "Minister of Liturgy." It is about church services, so I help the priests. In my school, I also organize the students to attend services every day, so I am training myself before joining the Carmelite sisters.

Here are greetings from Vincent, he is improving and he will soon complete his course. You know Mum I am only remaining with about seven months to complete my advanced level.

Mum you should always pray for me, as I always pray for you. In fact Mum I cannot sleep without offering you a prayer. Well Mum, I always pray so that one day we can see each other. I must come to your area. I know you don't have power to come to Uganda. Yet we need to see each other physically. I love you, Mum. I don't know how I can express my love for you. Only God knows how much we love each other. Greetings to Jack, I love him so much.

I wish you a nice stay filled with joy of all heavens.

From your beloved daughter,
Margaret

June 27, 2004

Dearest Margaret,

How can I explain the joy I have knowing that you have decided to join a Carmelite monastery! I pray for you and Vincent every day that God's highest graces will be given to you. I am so proud that you are taking your time to do AIDS counseling work. I am even more deeply proud that, with God's blessing, you too will become His bride in a few years. What better husband could you possibly have?

Pope John Paul II has said, "The Christian life is a life of penance and sacrifice." Christ said that we must take up our cross daily. I know you have done this a great deal already. St. Teresa of Avila, the early reformer of the Carmelite order, said that she did not want to see any sad-faced saints. Now, St. Thérèse of Lisieux took her predecessor's words to heart. One nun used to completely distract her. This happened day in and day out, and day in and day out. St. Thérèse was tempted to turn her head and give that nun a sour look. But she never did, out of love for that nun and Jesus. On washday, one nun felt St. Thérèse was not working hard enough, and she took a wash brush and tried to show her how to do it correctly. The clothes did not get much cleaner, but St. Thérèse got thoroughly wet, which she took with a smile. St. Thérèse always tried to meet everyone with a smile. There was one nun that could not stand St. Thérèse. No matter how mean she acted to St. Thérèse, St. Thérèse just smiled back to her. One day, this nun asked St. Thérèse, "What is it about me you like so much?" She told her that she saw in this nun the soul of Jesus. Margaret, this is all well and good.

Nuns in Carmelite monasteries are not sad; they are usually very joyous. There will be hard times and easy times. There will be time enough to become a saint. Whenever you have a problem, take it to God and our Mother Mary and ask the other sisters what you should do.

Jack says hello. He is very proud of you also. As a matter of fact, I always dictate your letters, and he types them up on our computer. I am fine relaxing on the bed with our dog lying beside me.

On February 13, I had an operation. Due to the doctor's error, I have not been off the bed since that time for anything except to go to the doctor's office in a wheelchair van. Weeks ago, the doctor told me to start exercising to rebuild my muscles. Yesterday, I stood up and held onto the sink from my wheelchair and then sat down. I did it two more times. My caregiver started applauding; the woman who is helping me with my exercises kept saying "Good job" many times, and Jack was massaging the back of my neck and shoulders. With all the congratulations, you would have thought I had been elected president of the United States, and I only spent six seconds standing up. I woke up today sore from the neck down and realized it was from standing up three times yesterday.

Today I was talking to God, and I asked Him for more faith. I had the television on and just then I looked up and saw "faith children's rosary." I just realized God had given me my faith. We must become like little children in faith and trust. When we say the rosary, we are being faithful. Margaret, He loves me, pampers me, is leading me home. Let us pray for each other.

I love you, dear heart, and so does Jack.

In the name of the Holy Spirit,
Mary Faith

October 18, 2004

Beloved Mum Mary Faith,

I thank the almighty God who has endeavored to give guidance and protection to your precious life. In fact, your life is so dangerous, and it's only God who can guide you and go through all the pains that you are receiving.

Mum, sorry for the operation that you went through in the last few months. I think you will be okay very soon through God's power. You should have in mind that suffering is par to the Christian life.

I was so surprised when in your previous letter you mentioned about sponsoring me for ten years. For sure, a mother cannot forget the date of birth of her child. In fact it is a long journey from my childhood, and now I am becoming a mature and a dignified young lady. For sure, when you began sponsoring me I started to be the happiest person in the whole world. Always the girls at school ask me whether I can become annoyed because whenever someone annoys me, I just reflect on your love and this helps me not get annoyed.

For the case of becoming a Carmelite, I am remaining with only two months and thereafter I will go and join the convent for sure. Becoming God's chosen person is a call from Him, and I think He called me. Also He has done great things to me and so I have to be His bride.

And I think with time I will also be a counselor to my fellow youths because the majority of the youths are still ignorant about the most killer disease, so we try different areas to enlighten the youths about the disease.

Mum, I have much to say, but send my greetings to Jack and the caregiver. I love them all and thank them for the love and care they are giving you.

Mum, have a nice stay and always put God in your midst. May the good Lord be with you.

I love you, Mum.

From your beloved daughter,
Margaret

December 26, 2004

Beloved Mum Mary Faith,

I greet you in the name of our Lord Jesus Christ.

I hope you are experiencing good changes in your health now. For this, I put trust in God. For me, things are still fine and a lot of good events have been occurring to me and the entire school. We had a workshop organized by the foundation concerning the future prospects. It was very profitable, since a lot was discussed. In addition, we had competitions in our school and my house, among the six houses, took the first position, and on October 9, 2004, we celebrated. I was the prefect for liturgy, and among all the forty-five prefects I was the most active and exemplary prefect. A lot of gifts were given to me and they were as follows, a very beautiful handbag, a flask, an album, shoes, a tray, and three certificates for leadership. This amuses my teachers and fellow students who were gathered around, including the head of the school, because all the prefects got only one gift and this was a challenge.

Once more, Mum, thank you for your ceaseless efforts and love you always take concerning my health and education. In fact, I cannot tell you how much you love me but it is only God who knows the love between you and me.

Thank you for the seventy-five dollars you sent to me. This amount of money was used for my necessities like buying shoes, clothes, and study tours. I am preparing to enter my vacation in

December. I hope a lot will be done during my vacation. And I have a desire to join the Carmelites on this vacation.

Allow me to stop here, since I am in a critical moment of doing my final examination. So I don't have much to tell you but I have greetings from my colleagues of the AIDS Club. They love you so much. I introduced you to them, they began to pray for you, and whenever they go to church, they take your photograph to the priest to pray for you by blessing the real photograph.

Mum, I love you so much and may the good Lord reward you abundantly for the work well done. May the almighty God bless you dear Mum. I love you, Mum.

All from your beloved daughter,
Margaret

2005

March 2, 2005

Beloved Mum Mary Faith,

I greet you in the name of our Lord Jesus Christ. How are you over there? I hope you are fine. Although Vincent and I are okay, we always say a special prayer every morning and evening for you. A gift from God and with Him all things are possible.

Let me take this opportunity to thank you for the twenty-five dollars you sent for my needs. You know during that period many people were starving. So much so, we had to buy a sack of rice and sugar. Till now, we have been depending on that. Indeed those people at home are proud of you. More so because I received the $100 for my graduation. For sure, I was so happy but I am still waiting for my examination to come back but we shall celebrate afterwards. Probably in March and I hope to send you some photographs. All in all, thank you very much for the love and sacrifice you do for me.

Always I ask myself this question, "What gift will I give to God?" Many people my age have not had this chance of acquiring enough knowledge. Instead they are in their villages producing children and even dying of AIDS. We have survived and thrived, which is a treasure. You know in my family we don't have a father and a mother but you are acting as both of them. You can imagine how lucky we are. We are so grateful for the support and being a hard-working Mum, because we are receiving whatever we feel like. May the almighty God protect you and bless you, and always reward you abundantly and even to add to whatever you possess.

Have a nice stay and here are greetings for Jack. I love him so much. I love you Mum.

From your beloved daughter,
Margaret

May 1, 2005

Dearest Margaret:

I am so joyful knowing that you have decided to join a Carmelite monastery! You are a fine young lady and Jack and I are so proud of you. Just a few years ago you were a little girl and now you are all grown up. I pray for you every day that God's highest graces will be given to you. Nuns in Carmelite monasteries are very joyous. As I have said, whenever you have a problem, take it to God and our Mother Mary, and ask the other sisters what you should do. Exactly when will you be entering the monastery and where is it located? Could you please send me the address so we can write to you? By the way, how is Vincent doing in his schooling?

I am also proud that you are taking your time to do AIDS counseling work. Pope John Paul II said, "The Christian life is a life of penance and sacrifice." Christ said that we must take up our cross daily, and I know you do this already. I want to thank you and all those who pray for me. You are such a blessing to me.

I am sure your examinations are all over, and I pray that you received good marks. Again, I am so proud of you and all you have done. I also pray that you are having good health and will continue so.

Jack says hello. He is very proud of you also. Let us pray for each other. I love you, Margaret, and I always will.

In the name of the Holy Spirit,
Your mum, Mary Faith

May 17, 2005

Dear Mary Faith,

Thank you for your recent inquiry. We visited with the child and here are her future plans:

Margaret informed us that she was advised by her parish priest to first pursue a degree at the university before she joins the monastery. She took the advice, and she is now looking for a university from where she will pursue her studies for four years. The university studies in Uganda opened in September, and we expect Margaret to start studies in September of this year. Margaret therefore expects to join the monastery in 2009 after she has completed her university studies. The child has written to you about these issues and the letter is in transit.

May the Lord continue blessing you.

June 15, 2005

Beloved Mum Mary Faith,

I take this opportunity to say a word of hello to you. Hope life is fine and the Lord continues to bless you.

Sorry for the death of our beloved Pope John Paul II, we had a Holy Mass on the day he was buried. It was led by the bishop. We thank God for the new pope he has given us.

With me life is well. I sat for my advanced level examinations and passed with 14 points. My wish has been to join the monastery now but my parish priest has advised me to first get a profession at the university and join the monastery afterwards. I have taken the advice of my Parish Priest and so dear Mum now I am looking for a university and I am hoping to take either of the following courses: bachelor of information technology or bachelor of arts with education. The studies at the university will take me four years. I am hoping to start classes in October this year and I shall be informing you about my progress.

My country is okay. We are awaiting the presidential elections next year. Already people are excited about the elections.

May the almighty God bless you and reward you abundantly. Greetings to Jack, I love him so much because he is your guide and protector.

From your beloved daughter,
Margaret

2006

April 2006

Dearest beloved Mum Mary Faith,

I take this opportunity to say a word of hi to you. Hope life is treating you well. I thank the almighty God who has protected your health.

On my side, life is not as good as I expected. Mum, I told you that I wanted to join the Carmelite community. We sat down with the people from the foundation to discuss my desire to become a Carmelite sister. They said it would be better to first get a degree at the university. They also said it would cost a lot of money, and the foundation could not afford it all. I decided that if the foundation could only give a little money to join the Carmelites community, it would be best. They refused to listen to my ideas. So now, I am still at home, can you imagine!

Mum, I was suggesting that if possible we could use the private means of communication, as we did years ago. I stay with my brother who decided to help me, if I join the Carmelite community. You can use his account number, which is in a rural bank. Even if it is a single coin, I can receive it without any fear. I want to join the Carmelites community, Mum.

Mum, I had thought that you are preparing to visit to Uganda. I suggest that if possible, we can go back together at your home area so that I can join the Carmelite sisters of your area (USA).

Lastly Mum, would you send me your email address. I will be grateful if all my requests are given your consideration. I love you, Mum, plus my dad, Jack. Thanks to him for having given you whatever you like. May the almighty God bless you and reward you in whatever you do.

The address you can use is on top of the envelope. That is

where I do charity work for the sick people, since I have not yet joined the Carmelite community.

I love you, Mum. I do not know what I can do to show you that I love you. Greetings to Jack.

From your beloved daughter,
Margaret

April 2006

Dear beloved Mum Mary Faith,

Greetings from your dearest daughter Margaret. It's good you are recovering from sickness. My side life is going on well. How is Dad?

Mum, it's a pleasure to write to you and explain more about joining the Carmelite community. In my last letter I had informed you how my parish priest advised me and I wished to take his advice on getting a profession before joining the community. However, I am now scared because the course I am taking of business administration costs nine hundred thousand per semester and yet the foundation can only afford three hundred thousand shillings per year. So now, Mum, I am worried whether I will attain my profession to enable me to join the Carmelites community, which I do greatly want. Let me end by wishing you nice stay as I continue praying to the almighty God to power on your riches glory and allow your life to continue with your generous heart. May god bless you.

From your beloved daughter,
Margaret

August 4, 2006

Dearest Margaret,

I will try to catch up on everything. First, I want to wish you a happy birthday, which is coming up.

It has been a long time since I last wrote to you. The doctors have been doing a lot of tests on me. They thought I might have a brain tumor, but now they don't think so. I hope you have recovered from the motorcycle accident and have no permanent problems from it. How do you feel in general?

I understand you are not in the university right now. I am so sorry you have not been able to enter the monastery there. I believe it is our Father in Heaven's plan for you. I talked to Sister Marya at the Springfield, Missouri, Carmelite monastery, which is approximately 155 miles away from me. She said that you should write a letter of intent to enter the monastery in Springfield, Missouri. Their address is: Carmel of Saint Anne, 424 Monastery Street, Springfield, Missouri, 65807.

I know all the sisters in Springfield. One is forty-five, one is sixty, and the prioress is older. In Springfield, the monastery is in a clean and wholesome part of town. They have many wonderful benefactors who give them many monetary donations, food and beverages, a TV set to watch religious programs, and basically whatever is needed at the time. The Carmel in Springfield is built of glass, wood, and brick. It is air-conditioned and heated. The bathroom is made of beautiful blue ceramic tile with individual places to shower. You would love it there.

We have a hurtle to get over. That is getting you a visa. The fastest you can come over is if you can find someone to sponsor you. I have had twenty operations. We are too poor now to sponsor you. So I suggest you seek the help of the sisters in Springfield to find a sponsor from one their benefactors for you. Oh, for the good old days, when I could buy you pretty dresses and reams of paper!

The visa card is also known as a green card. There is a lottery for a green card. In a visa lottery, a very large number of people combine their money, and from that group some names are drawn for visas. I am going to put some money into this lottery for you, Margaret. I hope you win.

Please continue to pray for me, and I will pray for you. How is Vincent doing? Please say hello for Jack and me.

I love you dearly and I miss you. Try to save souls. Become a saint, dear heart. Nothing else matters.

Again, happy birthday!

Love,
Mary Faith, your beloved mum

August 1, 2006

Dearest Mum Mary Faith,

I thank almighty God, who has given guidance and protection to your precious life. Your health is now improving, and God will continue to bless your life. I am happy that you are now feeling much better. Praise God.

I wrote to you last time about my joining the Carmelite monastery. I strongly wanted to join. I went to my parish priest, he told me to first join the university, which will take four years, and after that join the Carmelite monastery.

At the university, I am going to be on private sponsorship which is expensive because the tuition fee is six hundred thousand Ugandan shillings, accommodation and feeding three hundred thousand per semester. A semester is for six months. Mum, be assured that due to God's power, one day I will become one of the Carmelite sisters.

I love you, Mum, and I pray for you day and night because

you are the only one on this earth who is holding my future. Vincent is also doing well with his studies. Greetings to Jack, I love him so much. Have a nice stay filled with joy.

From your beloved daughter,
Margaret

October 20, 2006

Dearest Margaret,

I haven't heard from you, and the sisters in Springfield haven't either. I talked to Sister Marya, and she said they haven't heard from you at all. Do you still want to become a Carmelite nun, since it has been a dream of yours? The monastery in Springfield is not that far from me. I hope the priest didn't talk you out of your vocation and talk you into a college degree. With a college degree, you can help people. As a nun, you can save souls.

Reread St. Thérèse of Lisieux's autobiography where she talks about her desire as a child to offer herself up in love to God as a sacrificial offering to save souls. I thought that's what you wanted to do. I couldn't believe it when the priest talked you out of it. I don't want to force you to do something you don't want to do, but you always said that was what you wanted. All you needed was a sponsor. I think your vocation was swayed by the priest. If you have changed your mind, please let me know.

God bless you, and don't let me push you into a vocation you don't want. If you are able to come to the monastery, maybe you could come and see us. I can't wait to see you and give you a big hug and a kiss.

If you do have a vocation, apply to the Carmelite monastery and see about getting a visiting visa. I would love to see you.

Love and kisses,
Mary Faith, your mum

December 2006

Beloved Mum Mary Faith,

I first want to express my feelings of joy and happiness to hear from you. As on the side of your daughter, I am fairly good. I am busy reading books so I can get a first class degree.

I received your letter in which you asked me whether I still feel I have a vocation to join the Carmelite sisters. Dear Mum, I feel I am going to disappoint you. I have had a change of mind concerning my vocation. A year ago, I got a boyfriend, we are in love with one another, and we plan to marry after I have completed my first degree at the university. I am sorry to hurt your feelings. All those are God's plan and wishes.

Mum, I love you and I always think and pray for you day and night. I had a sleepless night praying for your good health, I always pray to St. Jude, because he is known for performing miracles. Mum, have you ever sat down and thought about how much I love you?

Allow me to wish the almighty God be with you in whatever you do. I love you, Mum.

From your beloved daughter,
Margaret

December 2006

Dear beloved Mum Mary Faith,

Here are greetings from your daughter, Margaret. I love you, Mum. How is life over there on your side? I am very okay after surviving a motorcycle accident. Thank you for your prayers and love. They helped a lot. I always pray for you, too.

Vincent is doing great, and he sends regards to you. He, too, is pursuing a course at the university.

Recently, there was a strike at the university. Lecturers laid down their tools, because they want their salaries increased. In return the students rioted because they could not go to class, even though they paid tuition. The government decided that the university should be closed. However, the issue is still under debate. We are worried, but pray and hope that it will not close until we finish with the semester exams. Chaos is everywhere … oh!!

God loves you, so do I. You are in the prayers of someone who cares. Kind regards to Jack. I can hear the Christmas bells singing. It reminds me Christmas is almost here.

Merry Christmas and Happy New Year 2007.

Lots of love, your beloved Daughter,
Margaret

2007

February 7, 2007

Dearest Margaret,

It's been a long time since I received your letter, but this letter is one of congratulations to you and your boyfriend and on your studies. Tell me about your boyfriend. I assume you will be married in the church. I still have my wedding dress, and maybe you would like to wear it. It is satin and lace with a lace veil. It would make me so happy if you would accept it. Mothers often give their daughters their wedding dress. We have had it stored for years. It will be ready for you to slip on for your wedding. I can't believe my little Margaret is all grown up.

For ten years you and I have thought you would be a Carmelite nun; but if you ever want to be a nun, there are easier orders. Just because you don't want to be a Carmelite nun doesn't mean you can't go to another order where there are young people.

Christ said a man can't love another person more than to give his life for another. That is a saint and that is what Jack has done for me. He has given up his life, especially since I have been crippled. Please pray for my husband that he will become a saint, become a Catholic, and receive the blood of Christ. Jack does not know what he is missing like you and I know, Margaret. Another reason I hope your husband is a Roman Catholic is because there is nothing lonelier than being in a pew without your husband.

Whatever you do, please stay a Catholic, no matter if you are single or married. All you need to work for is being a saint. Stay close to the body and blood of Christ, and go to Mass, and say the rosary. There have been married saints but put God first, then your husband, then your work. I hope I am leaving you a legacy in this letter. Maybe this letter will give you some insight.

Margaret, I bet you are like I was when Jack and I were dating. All I could think about was Jack, even when I was at work. Tell me all about your boyfriend and studies. Are you going to teach? I'm so happy you are in love; so am I. I'm in love with a wonderful God and a wonderful guy. How about you?

Love,
Your most beloved mum, Mary Faith

April 15, 2007

Dearest Mum Mary Faith,

I greet you in the name of our Lord Jesus Christ. How is life over there? On my side life is good, only I am so busy with the university books.

Here is good news to tell you that I was promoted to the second semester of the university. Hope to be qualified as a professional teacher two years to come. I am reading hard so that I can get a first class degree. In Jesus name, I will get it.

I have been sick for two weeks ago but I recovered thanks to the Lord because I am now looking healthy. How is life, Mum? How was Christmas and Easter celebrations? Hope they were so enjoyable.

Allow me to pen off. I love you as I love myself. May God bless all your good work you do towards me. I am very appreciative.

May God keep you very safely.

From your beloved daughter,
Margaret

Emails

2007

August 27, 2007

Margaret and Vincent, I love you, I love you, I love you, I love you, I love you, I love you, I love you, I love you, I love you, I love you, I love you, I love you, I love you, I love you, I love you. I just said what you said to me when you called me on the phone. I will send you some money through the Christian Foundation for Children and Aging as an emergency need.

Back to you, Margaret. Happy, happy birthday, Margaret. We have been together since you were eleven years old. And now you are a grown woman. We have been together for thirteen years. Thanks to all your hard work on your studies, you are well educated and speak, think, read, and write English.

Jack has said that you can live with us for some time. Please do not get too excited about this right now. However, you are in our will.

In Christ's name and love,
Your devoted mum, Mary Faith

August 28, 2007

Perhaps you can tell me what kind of visa you want me to apply for. Would it be a long visiting visa or a school visa? I really don't know anything about visas. Where do I go to contact someone about a visa?

Margaret, Dad Jack and I are living from one paycheck to another. We have enough, I believe, to welcome you to our home with open arms. We both want you to live with us. I cannot wait to see you in person. Can it be that after all these years, I will see you in person, will be able to hug and kiss you?

I give you, Margaret, and Vincent all my love. So does Dad Jack. God bless both of you. May He give you both His special graces and blessings. Pray to our Lady.

With love from your mum, Mary Faith Holzer

August 30, 2007

Beloved Mum,

I am so happy that you are okay, thanks for your lovely text, I can't wait to see you in person, Mum. About the visa or air ticket, try to contact this website http://www.americanembassey.com. I would like to stay and live with you Mum and Dad Jack! Mum, let me also go to our American embassy in Uganda to collect more information. After that, I'll send you a copy of the information I would have gotten there.

With that, Mum, greetings to you and Dad Jack and I love you all.

Hope Mum my dreams will come true.

God bless you all, your beloved daughter
Margaret Namiiro

August 30, 2007

My dearest Margaret,

I would like to send you $100 USD. In one of your letters, you mentioned that there might be a way to do a bank transfer from my bank account to Vincent's bank account.

Can you tell me if that is possible and do you want to do that?

I cannot wait to hear from you again. I have learned a person can finish getting a teacher's degree online. It is possible to get financial aid for these online degrees. I ran into one school that allowed people with visas (green cards) to be accepted for funding.

Another school only allowed US citizens to apply for financial aid.

Did I tell you I have an invention? This invention will help many elderly and disabled people. I certainly hope I can help my daughter, Margaret.

I love you from the depth of my heart, my darling Margaret.

From your mum, Mary Faith

September 3, 2007

My beloved, brilliant, beautiful, knowledgeable, and wonderful daughter,

Does it sound like I am mad at you? No, not even a little, little bit. Yes, I love you fifteen times over. I can, unfortunately, put my knowledge about visas in a sewing thimble. However, I was not sure about it. Do you know how long you can visit Dad Jack and me? Will you please find out? Also, in your next email, will you also give me your address? I definitely want you to come as soon as possible. I need your address before I can call the airlines about your ticket.

Margaret, I have had twenty-two operations. I am okay, but one operation has left me crippled, and I need to see doctors occasionally. I am truly okay, and when I start selling the book, then you can come and stay with Dad Jack and me. There is always room in the home when there is room in the heart. I want to have you as long as I can. Church is only two blocks away. I love you so much, I cannot wait to hear from you again. I keep checking my mail for something from you, darling daughter.

How is Vincent? I would love to get a real chance to talk to him. How are you and Vincent spending your time? Whatever it is, you are good Catholics, and I know I would like it. Much love in Christ, our Savior.

Your mum,
Mary Faith.

September 10, 2007

Dearest Mum,

How is it going? Hope you're okay! How is Dad Jack? We are okay. Can I tell you something mum? The queen of England is coming to Uganda one week from now, the country is very busy, so Mum, tell me what's going on in USA. Here everything is fine, how is Dad Jack doing? Tomorrow, Mum, I am sending my photo to you. Mum, do you still receive letters from the project? I wanted to know because am no longer there. I am independent and no one should send you any letter from that organization. Mum, there are some reasons why I left that organization, of which I can't tell them to you now, Mum.

Do you want to learn my language? Greeting someone in the morning we say "wasuze otya no," meaning that it is a good morning. Mum, I joined the rotary club. It's good, we always find new people whenever we go for different meetings and activities like looking for the needy in areas being affected by wars and assisting the church in the services. I love you, Mum, greetings to Dad Jack.

Your beloved Margaret

September 10, 2007

Dearest and beloved Margaret, darling, are you working for the nearby chemical plant? We are still sending the project twenty-five dollars a month for you; are you receiving the money from them?

Margaret, I have always tried to give you unconditional love. You do not have to worry about my disapproval. I love you no matter what has happened. You have made me interested in why you left the project. When you come here, we can go to church together. If you find a good Catholic to fall in love with and marry in the church, you will automatically become a citizen. Do not decide on marriage just to become a citizen. You would be unhappy. But now all should be happiness. Dad Jack and I are going to see and love you in person.

Margaret, when you receive this, and you have some time, call me collect. I will get the bill. Just call the operator. Tell her you want to "make a collect call to anyone who answers" (it is cheaper than calling person to person) at our number. I will be charged.

You will pay nothing.

Your mum

September 12, 2007

Darling Mum,

Thank you for the message you sent me. Mum, about the money you always send to the project. I no longer get it from there, like over a year now. Please Mum, I am suggesting that the money be saved for my AIR ticket. Yes am working near that chemical firm. Now, Mum, about the invitation letter, I have enclosed the format of the letter I should present to the American embassy. Use that exact letter, change some words, then send the letter. Or perhaps Dad Jack could inquire about this. The embassy people need proof I am invited. How is Dad Jack? I hope he is okay.

Mum, I've to go to lunch here in Uganda. The time is 2:00 pm. I hope you are in bed, Mum. Good night, Mum. Greetings to Dad Jack. Tell him that I love him. May God bless you all.

Your daughter, Margaret

September 15, 2007

My darling Margaret,

British Airways, which services both Africa and the USA, has a very big sale on airline tickets. I am expecting an unknown amount of money from a two- to three-year lawsuit. The lawsuit is against a drug that gave me diabetes while I was taking the drug. I should find out how much I will receive at the end of this month. I should receive the money, if I get any, in October. Please pray for your airfare plus some other large amount I need. You can stay in my country forever and start citizenship classes if you are being persecuted. One such example of this is war such as the one against Catholics in Uganda.

You said you were in a safe place, but perhaps not. If that war is still going on, you are Catholic and could be killed from a long way away. Perhaps you are being persecuted.

What caused the loss of your job? Catholic persecution? Do you understand me, Margaret? You can also strengthen your chance to come if, besides an invitation from us, you want to study. Please answer all my questions: airport city, persecution in any form, desire to study.

I love you, my daughter, as always in Christ.

Your mum, Mary Faith

September 19, 2007

Dearest Mum,

I am so so sorry for not writing back to you in time because I've been sick for three days, it was the flu. How is Dad Jack? How is home? About this question, "What caused the loss of your job ... Catholic persecution?" Mum, the answer is yes, because of overexploitation, meaning they used not to pay us yet we were overworked. We worked from morning to evening. Mum, was I wrong to leave the job? Mum, about the invitation letter, should it be a visitation letter so that when I get there I'll change everything to a study visa?

Mum, about the war, it was there for some time back, but now we are in a safe place.

Back to you, Mum. How are you? Greetings from Vincent. He loves you. I wish you a nice day with all God's blessings. I LOVE YOU, MUM & DAD JACK.

From your beloved Margaret

September 22, 2007

Sweet Mum, how are you and Dad Jack?

Back to me, I am okay. Beloved mother, whenever I lie [sleep] on my bed I dream about you, and afterwards I pray to St. Jude the apostle to make my dreams come true. Mum, St. Jude is always besides me and is there for me like my dearest mum. Vincent is doing well and he says that he loves you one hundred times. In Uganda we are in the rainy season and many people are affected by floods and so they are looking for safe places. Mum, right now I work as a shop attendant near the chemical plant but the job is not good, Mum, because I get very little salary and yet I work from morning to evening. Mum, what can I do? Should I leave the job?

Darling mother, I wish you a nice day filled with joy of all heavens. May the almighty God bless you.

From your daughter, Margaret

September 22, 2007

Dearest Margaret,

When I worked, I worked very hard at every job I had. There were some jobs I worked that were just like what you are describing now. My advice, since you asked for it, is to not leave your present job until you find a better job, then you will always have at least some money coming in until you find that great job.

Do you remember the letter that I wrote to you when you were trying to decide what your vocation was to be? Now that you speak English and have, I believe, two years of college, you can apply to be a flight attendant with an airline. You are also qualified to work in hotel management and give hospitality to tourists. But to do this, you need to be where the airplanes are, such as Entebbe. If Entebbe has an airport, surely it has good hotels. Being a flight attendant would be a job you would love and you would get to see the world, or at least part of it, before you come here.

When you go to apply for these jobs, wear a suit and slightly high heels. Please do not cover your beautiful hair with anything. Sell yourself to your next job interviewer. Tell him why he should hire you, but not too bluntly. Be confident in his eyes, even if you are shaking inside. Make your job interviewer think you are his best choice. You need to be sure of yourself, but not so much so that you are cocky or overly confident.

I also think a good job would be to work for an airline at the ticket counter. That way, you could familiarize yourself with the airport in Entebbe before you fly out of there to come here. Try to work for British Airways if you can. I am almost certain you can easily work yourself up to a free flight (such as to the Holzer home in the United States). I just asked Dad Jack if this is true, and he said, "Yes, this is a good idea. My friend, Dave, used to get free tickets all the time." Please answer me in your next email.

Did you get a long email that told you about how you will come here from Entebbe using British Airways to the state of Texas in the United States? From Texas you will fly a fairly short trip to MCI Airport, where Dad Jack and I will pick you up.

Take any job you can get with British Airways, but try working at the ticket counter first and flight attendant second. The third job offered by British Airways, take it, so you can get a free ticket.

When you are interviewing, and after you get a job, do not tell anyone you are planning on leaving the job to come here. That would be the best way to *not* get the job or to lose the job. You could tell a woman friend, and she could tell management who might think of drummed up reason to fire you.

Dad Jack wants to see if he can do a test to see if you can receive cash through the mail. He wants to try an amount of twenty-five dollars first. Then, I believe, he will try a larger amount. He needs your current address.

Margaret, I think St. Jude just answered your prayers! How far away is Entebbe from you? When you come here, you will fly out of Entebbe Airport on British Airways. I love you with all my heart, darling, and I always will. Pray that the money from my lawsuit is large, because Dad Jack said you can come stay if I can pay for it, because he cannot afford it due to all our bills. Remember, Dad Jack loves you! Is there any way Vincent can go to Entebbe with you? I do not want to break up a winning team. Tell Vincent hello, and that we love him.

To both of you, blessed be the name of Christ.

September 29, 2007

Beloved Mother,

How are you and Dad Jack? I hope you are okay. Mum, thank you for the wonderful idea you sent to me, in fact I have tried my level best to make a research in those different jobs you mentioned, like working at the ticket counter, and the manager told me that it is not easy for someone to get a job quickly. In this case, one has to write an application letter, you keep on checking over one to two years, and after you may get a chance to go for an interview. He told me that many people apply for those jobs and worst of all, in Uganda we have "technical know-how," meaning that jobs are given to those who have relatives in those areas. Poor Margaret doesn't have any relatives that can get her a job there.

Mum, about the issue of Dad using the mail to send me money, may not be good, and so I was suggesting that let Dad use my *bank* address to send me money. I can receive it without any worry. Sweet mum, you wanted to know the distance between Entebbe and my residence. It is 20 km. The distance is not too far accordingly. Allow me to end here. I love you with all my heart. Greetings from Vincent. He loves you. May the almighty one bless and be with you always.

From Margaret, your daughter

September 29, 2007

Margaret, my beautiful, darling daughter,

I would not believe the person who told you that once you get your application in, then you have to wait so long. Margaret, didn't I send you to a good parochial school? A private school? You have more education than probably 98 percent of the other people in Uganda. Please apply for a study visa, if it is all right with you. Father Denis studied over here for three years. You also are fluent in English. I think that the person was jealous of you and trying to demoralize you. Perhaps he does not believe in women working at all.

I think you could work for an airline in Entebbe if you could move there and you were not too far away from Vincent. Take any job that pays well and you can get at an airline. Or, look for hospitality work or any other suitable work in a hotel. Be confident and tell the management about your background in English. Convince the people they need you more than you need them.

In regard to studying over here, I will try to put you in school on the computer. You never go to a campus, you do your schoolwork online at my house, and you can get a degree in fifteen to eighteen months. Do not tell the visa people you will only be studying for eighteen months yet, because you cannot know this positively. Let the visa people assume 3 or 4 years.

Thank you for praying very hard about the lawsuit. From what I have been told by the lawyers, I should receive a good amount. I am planning on paying for your computer schooling, which is only part-time.

I love you seventy times seven (the perfect number). Dad Jack loves you a lot too.

Give our love to Vincent. Please keep praying about the lawsuit.

Yours in the love of Christ, your mum

October 5, 2007

Hello sweet Mum,

How are you over there, are you okay? I pray to the almighty God to continue to protect and guide you always. How is Dad Jack? Mum, I was in one of the best schools in Uganda, but in this country the process of getting a job is very different from yours. In this case people with high qualifications like managers give only to their relatives. That is the country we are living in, Mum. I have no one to assist me to get a job here.

Secondly, darling mum, try your level best and send me the invitation letter using the mail, before I can apply for the visa. I will be able to print it out and present it to the American Embassy (visa people). Remember, the invitation letter is very useful since it contains more information about you (area, city, etc.). Mum, you can use a study visa in your invitation letter and how long it will take. Am eagerly waiting for the invitation letter. It was good to hear that am going to be studying on the computer at your home as I get my degree. That is marvelous. Thank you for the care and love you always render to me.

Allow me to end here. I wish you all the best.

May God bless you with His spirit. I love you all.

Your daughter, Margaret

October 5, 2007

Dearest, beloved Margaret,

It has been a long time since we have heard from you. Dad Jack would like the name and full address of your bank so he can send you an experimental twenty-five dollars to start. Please send the name and address as soon as possible, so you can get the first experimental money. I believe Jack wants to send you more later, if you get this first amount all right.

Are you trying to find a job in Entebbe? Did you get my last letter? Darling, am I being of help to you? I would hate to think I am being a hindrance to you. You are always on my mind and heart. I really do have the deep, deep love of a mother toward a daughter. I do not want to hurt you in any way ever.

Please continue to pray about the lawsuit. I called one of the lawyers to see if we won the case and to understand how much each one would receive. Because I had called twice more in a period of months, the lawyer gave me the brush-off and said that all the lawyers were trying to figure out how much everyone was going to get in a period of several weeks, but they could work faster if they didn't get so many calls. I had to tell her I would not call again. I felt like you must feel sometimes. I felt put down and not able to do anything about it. I noticed before she said all the claimants would receive a check in October and now she is saying in several weeks. That may mean that it could take all October and then some weeks after that. I imagine a large number of people are calling her.

Dearest Margaret, please pray that I will receive a large amount of money for several important reasons, such as having money for my invention, which will help the elderly and disabled, and the most important reason is to have my beautiful daughter, Margaret, to stay with us until at least she becomes a United States citizen. I love you as much as any mother can, dear heart.

In the love of the Trinity,
Mary Faith and Dad Jack

October 13, 2007

Hi, sweet Mum,

How are you? I am okay and here are greetings from Vincent. He always prays for you and he loves you so much plus Dad Jack. I don't have much to say. I love you all, may God bless you always. Have a nice day filled with joy.

Margaret

October 18, 2007

Dear Margaret,

I am sending this email to you because Dad Jack has given up trying to get the address of the Western Union office near you.

He loves you and knows you and Vincent love him, which he is glad to hear. However, he is frustrated that you do not send the Western Union address. I feel you must have some kind of job or you would answer our questions in order to get money.

We will send twenty-five dollars through Western Union in order to make sure we are able to get money to you. Please tell the address and anything else we need to know about sending to this Western Union now. Also, tell me how you are supporting yourself. We have been trying to send money to you for a long time but cannot without your help. I love you and always will.

Mary Faith, your mum

October 24, 2007

Beloved Mother,

How are you? I always pray for you because of your help, support, and love you render to me. God is the only person who can know the reward he will give you. In addition to that in our country you may find only 2 percent of the people can give that love to the poor.

About the Western Union in this country, the Western Union is the easiest means of money transfer. The following are needed, the country: Uganda, city: Kampala, name of the person you are sending money too, and the amount of money. So I will just go to any nearby Western Union and withdraw the money.

Mum, my way of surviving is not good at all. You know I stay with my youngest sister who I have to give support, like getting what to eat, and yet I get a little money. Sometimes I fail to get what to eat and we only take tea but we are happy. I love you all, may God bless you all.

From your daughter,
Margaret

October 26, 2007

Beloved and dearest Margaret,

Now you can go to any Western Union in Kampala and withdraw twenty-five dollars. Margaret, as far as I know, you have one brother, Vincent. What do you mean when you say that you are staying with your sister? This is only a question, not an indictment. I will always love you. I will love you unconditionally now and throughout all eternity.

Unfortunately, payment from the lawsuit has been put off until sometime after the first of the year. We are not prosperous. We will have to wait on bringing you over until we get the lawsuit money. Remember that according to Romans, in the Bible, "*All things work to the good for those that love God.*" We just have to postpone a little all the hugs and kisses that I want to give you over here, and all those hugs and kisses I want from you.

In His love,
Your mum, Mary Faith

November 2, 2007

Dearest Margaret,

Did you receive the twenty-five dollars we sent to the Western Union office in Kampala? Jack has sent it.

Many years ago, after your natural mother and father had died, you told me there were only you and Vincent in your family. Where did the sister you said you are staying with come from?

Since you have had jobs in the near past that work day and night, Jack and I knew you could not do this and study at the university. Therefore we asked the project for some of our money back. We received a curt reply from Father Denis that you were going to school. He knew this because you had given him three receipts from school, and because you were still in the project. He also said we could only correspond through letters sent to the project.

Margaret, it is long overdue that we all, including myself, listen to you and what you want for your life. I will listen very carefully to you. You are not too old for anything you want to do. Just pray over this to God and our blessed Mother to help you decide what you want to do.

This is the most important time in your life. Before Jesus did anything big, he prayed.

Whatever my Margaret decides to do, I will do my best to help you.

I love you and always will.

Your mum, Mary Faith

November 5, 2007

Dearest Dad Jack,

How are you? Good news! I have received the twenty-five dollars you sent to me. I was worried that the money was stolen. But, praise the Lord, I received the amount you sent safely. It was through your love and care that I got to receive that money. Thanks you for not giving up, Dad. I love you and always pray for you.

All from your daughter,
Margaret

Printed in the United States
by Baker & Taylor Publisher Services